AF326795

Independent Publishing

Andrew L. Simon

Simon Publications
2002

Library of Congress Control Number: 2001119350

ISBN: 1-931541-99-X

Published by Simon Publications Inc., P.O.Box 321, Safety Harbor, FL 34695

"He who first shortened the labor of Copyists by device of *Movable Types* was disbanding hired Armies and cashiering Kings and Senates and creating a whole new Democratic world: He has invented the Art of printing."

Thomas Carlyle (1795 - 1881)

What would Carlyle say today about electronic printing that placed the enormous power of publishing into the hands of each and every citizen?

Contents

Introduction

From my childhood, I was afflicted with a serious case of bibliophilia. From Sinclair's *Lanny Budd* to Forester's *Hornblower* series, I devoured everything at an early age. Later, for some compelling reason that, in retrospect, is now immaterial, I became an engineer. Being congenitally lazy, I ended up to be a university professor. Life went on.

Throughout thirty years in the faux-ivory towers of academia, the publishing business fascinated me. Peripherally, I had many contacts with it. As an engineering department head for twenty-seven years, salesmen representing all major publishers paid visits each semester. They peddled their new textbooks for adaption in our courses, filled my bookshelves with free review copies, took me out to lunch, and stroked my ego with questions: "Do you have a project in mind? — When do you write a book for us?"

I did set out one time, just for fun, to write a little book on the worldwide history of weights and measures. Sounds boring, I now admit, but how else can you learn that the length of a Chinese mile, the *li*, depends on whether you go uphill or downhill? Come to think of it, it does make sense. I wrote it long-hand on endless stapled sheets of yellow legal pads. Proofreading, retyping, eliminating the new typos went on like migraine headache. Finally, copies were made and were sent to a group of publishers. It was a skinny little manuscript. The rejection letters stacked higher.

After a while, in the early 1970s, I received an encouraging phone call from a New York publisher of well-known field guides. It did, in a small way, changed my life. The caller was a Mrs. Wilson —bless her heart, wherever she is— onetime science teacher in North Carolina turned editor at this publishing firm. She announced her visit to Ohio to discuss my publishing proposal. Heady stuff it was, at the time. Later, during our occasional encounters, she regaled me with tales from the business of publishing. She has done a number of free-lance projects in children's literature and published over twenty books by that time. She told me, for instance, about a fellow whose career interest stopped short at bicycling. With Mrs. Wilson's help, he wrote a book on the subject, moved to Florida to live on his royalties, biking around.

It sounded more alluring than going to meetings with pompous professors or grading papers. I was hooked.

The oil crisis in 1974 presented my first opportunity to publish. From friends at Goodyear Aerospace (Loral today) I got access to a fine collection of books and newspaper clippings on energy resources. Using this data, I set out writing my first book, *Energy Resources.* It was published by the venerable Pergamon Press in 1976. It received a lot of positive reviews, but economic success it was not. At the time, by the way, the owner of Pergamon Press was the notorious publishing titan Robert Maxwell, who later was lost at sea from his yacht. Soon after his disappearance, the retirement funds of his employees was also announced to be lost, but not at sea.

On many occasions I met impressive people working in the publishing world. They were publishers and editors of big firms, in other industries they would have been called vice-presidents and managers. They told fascinating tales. Most of them worked on the side, publishing books, free-lance style. Apparently, there was money to be made in the publishing business, and they had the insiders' knowledge and understanding of how it is done.

I learned that it is possible to make big money on college textbooks. The author of a book I used in a course earned over $100,000 each year in royalties. It was almost twice my yearly income at the time. Authors of thousand-page texts used in required courses on general topics like Western Cultural Traditions make a great deal more money. With some fifteen million college students in America, fifteen percent royalty can be a gold mine from a well-written college textbook bought by hordes of students.

To my great surprise I also found out that the big publishing firms —McGraw-Hill, Wiley, Prentice-Hall, and the rest— are not as megalithic as they appear. Their publishers, editors and business staff are supported by myriads of independent, free-lance copy editors, graphic artists, designers, and proofreaders. Once I asked a high-ranking publisher friend at McGraw-Hill why most of these companies are located in New York City. He answered; "this is where the people we depend on live." So publishers and editors live in classy Stamford and Greenwich, Connecticut, and the artists and other free-lance help live in bohemian Greenwich Village.

While most books were designed by these assorted professionals in the United States, they were typeset abroad, in countries like Ireland, Hong Kong, Singapore. It was globalization, before its time.

Prestigious Wiley published my first engineering textbook, *Hydraulics* in 1976. It was translated to Spanish and Chinese and was used as a college text all over the world. It was ego-boosting to meet with graduate students from Peru and South Korea who studied from my book as undergraduates at home. The book went through four editions. After the third edition Prentice-Hall bought the copyright. They published the fourth edition, doubled the price and peddled it to an entirely wrong audience. Not surprisingly, royalty checks soon shriveled, demonstrating that even a huge publisher could do stupid things. There wasn't much to do about it. Writers were the peons of the publishers, with their rights signed away for eternity.

By the late 1980s, as computer technology advanced on all fronts. Fundamental changes loomed ahead for the whole publishing industry. Desktop publishing, computerized typesetting, electronic printing, and computer graphics were gradually replacing the traditional methods. Here are two illustrations for this transition, from my personal experience:

In 1998, I was commissioned to write a book entitled *Made in Hungary*. It took over 2,000 hours to complete it on a PC, with desktop publishing software, and it was printed using traditional printing technology. The cost of printing 2,500 copies exceeded $10,000.

Two years later, I wrote and published *The College Racket*, a critical overview of America's college degree manufacturing industry. The cost of setting up that book in the computer of the newly established electronic printing company was under $200. With print-on-demand technology —a new development— the author/publisher pays for the cost of printing as the orders for copies arrive. No heavy investment is necessary anymore for printing and warehousing thousands of unsold copies.

Empowered with this new technology, in 2001 my wife and I have republished nearly 200 classic books on history[1] that were out of print for many decades. Today, they are offered on all online booksellers and are sold through major book wholesalers.

The creative freedom associated with desktop publishing and electronic printing is tantamount to a cultural revolution. Authors will no longer be subjected to the intellectual restraint and commercial control of publishers and their editors as they were in the past. The literary marketplace will never again be dominated by a few influential media giants. It is now open to anyone. Each and every citizen has access to it. It is a powerful force. Let us hope that people will use it wisely, in a responsible, moral and dignified way.

1   http://www.simonpublications.com

Independent Publishing

Publishing Then and Now

When I wrote my first published book, *Energy Resources,*[1] no one dreamed of personal computers, gigabytes of memory, printers, scanners and optical character recognition. With early 1970s technology, writing a book entailed the use of an electric typewriter— preferably equipped with an ultra-modern correcting tape cartridge— scissors and Scotch-tape, pages with handwritten corrections all over. When the finished manuscript came back from the typist, it was usually full of errors. The cycle of cutting, pasting, adding and correcting was repeated again and again, until the ultimate version, neatly typed, was sent to a potential publisher.

Common courtesy required in those days that a manuscript be sent to only one publisher at a time. This, however, was rarely followed. Sending out a dozen copies was not unheard of. Once the manuscript was sent, the waiting began. Often rejections arrived by return mail. Longer waits meant sometime that the manuscript was considered seriously by the acquisition editor of the publishing company and copies were sent out to reviewers. Then again, the package may have been sitting on a secretary's desk waiting for the next round of rejections. Persis-

---

1   Andrew L. Simon: *Energy Resources*, New York: Pergamon Press, 1975

tent authors had ample opportunity to paper their den with rejection letters.

Writers of first novels or other fiction didn't even have an opportunity to approach a publisher directly. They worked through literary agents. They still do. Agents can supply editorial guidance, advise on career strategy, and —in the increasingly fluid and unpredictable world of modern publishing— provide the author a degree of continuity. What agents cannot be expected to do is to comment at length on unsuitable work or sell the unsaleable. Nor can they guarantee that the writer's life is without disappointments. The primary task of a literary agent is to look after the writer's commercial interests and to exploit fully the rights in the material he or she handles. This can mean anything from placing work with a publisher to the sale of foreign rights, translation, dramatic, film, television, audio, electronic and other rights.

Some agents do charge an author a reading fee, others do not. Those who charge a fee, which includes a written report, usually refund it upon a publisher's acceptance of the manuscript.

As the great majority of large publishers are headquartered in New York City, most literary agents are located there also. Hence, fiction writers can easily find themselves an agent in the Manhattan telephone directory. If a literary agent was willing to take on a aspiring author, the latter had to sign away 10 to 15 percent of the expected royalties for the effort of the agent toward finding a willing publisher. But even finding an agent who would represent a budding author is hard. Good literary agents are picky. Without their assistance, getting a publisher for a book is difficult. This doesn't necessarily mean that the manuscript is bad. Dr. Seuss's first book was rejected by 27 publishers. John Grisham's first book was rejected by twelve. He started out by self-publishing and selling his first book, *A Time to Kill,* out of the trunk of his car. *Twelve Golden Threads* by Aliske Webb was rejected by 150 publishers. After printing them on her own and selling 25,000 copies, she signed a four-book contract with HarperCollins. J. K. Rowling's first manuscript, *Harry Potter and the Sorcerer's Stone,* was rejected by all major British publishing houses before Bloomsbury offered a contract and a £ 2,500 advance. By the end of 2001, her books were translated into 42 languages and over hundred million copies were sold, making Rowling one of the richest persons in Britain.

Non-fictional books, like college textbooks, do not require an agent. With such a project, a qualified author contacts the acquisition editor of a publishing house directly.

Receiving a publishing contract based on an outline and a few chapters is a big day in the life of a new 'author,' even though the contract just spells out that the publisher will print a *publishable* manuscript. What is publishable will ultimately be determined by the publisher. Non-fiction books, such as college texts or monographs are first sent to reviewers who are presumably familiar with the subject matter. On occasion such reviews are constructive. But some reviewers are lazy and their critique is worthless. Other reviewers, who plan to write their own books in the same field, do their best to torpedo a potential competitor or steal some of his ideas.

The financial part of a typical publishing contract is difficult for a new author to fathom. The author of a non-fictional book, such as a college text usually gets 15 percent of the list price for classroom adaptions, but may be only 5 percent from "trade" sales, such as through a bookstore. Book-club sales, foreign rights, mail order sales and translations into foreign languages all involve different royalty percentages, usually small numbers. These are generally negotiable. But a new author is so happy to have a signed publishing contract at hand that he or she will be willing to sign anything just to be a 'published author,' without arguing about the fine print of the contract.

As an example, a rather typical publishing agreement used by one of the world's major scientific publishing houses is shown below:

PUBLISHING AGREEMENT

AGREEMENT made this date, between XXXX, (hereinafter called the "Publisher") and

X.Y.   Address......   (hereinafter called the "Author")

1.   Agreement to Publish

The Author agrees to prepare for publication by the Publisher, and the Publisher agrees to publish, a work provisionally entitled:

Title: ....

(hereinafter called the "Work") subject to the terms and conditions specified in this Agreement.

When the Author is more than one person, the word "Author" as used in this Agreement will apply collectively unless otherwise indicated. Each co-author will be bound by all provisions of this Agreement, and unless otherwise specified, all co-authors will share equally in all benefits and all obligations of this Agreement.

2.   Rights Granted

The Author hereby grants and assigns to the Publisher the full and exclusive rights comprising the copyright of the Work and all revisions thereof, including, but not limited to, the right to publish and distribute the Work and to prepare, publish and distribute derivative works based thereon in English and in all other languages, throughout the World, in all forms and media of expression now known or developed in the future, and to license or permit others to do so, during the term of copyright and all extensions, renewals and revisionary periods thereof.

The Publisher will register the Work in the Copyright Office of the United States in its own name in compliance with the U.S. copyright law and the Universal Copyright Convention.

3.   Material Preparation and Delivery

a)   The Author agrees to deliver to the Publisher no later than (date), two copies of the manuscript of the Work as described below, all of which will be acceptable to the Publisher in content and form. If the Author anticipates being unable to make timely delivery of the Work, the Author will so inform the Publisher in writing, and the Publisher may then agree to another date or may terminate this Agreement, as described below.

b)   The manuscript will consist of:

        i)   Approximately XXX pages of text, tabular matter and bibliography suitable for use as printer's copy,

        ii)   approximately XX black-and-white photographs, line drawings and diagrams suitable for direct reproduction, any necessary electronic files or materials, diskettes, CD-ROM masters, or audio/video masters.

c)   The manuscript will be delivered in an electronic format acceptable to the Publisher TeX, LaTeX, or an equivalent program.

d)   If the manuscript contains any material protected by the copyright of others, the Author will deliver to the Publisher with the manuscript written permission from the copyright owner to utilize such material in the Work. The Author will be responsible for any costs that may be associated with obtaining such permission.

e)   If the Author fails to deliver any of the above-mentioned material ready for production by the date specified above (unless extended), or if the material, as delivered, is not acceptable in content and in form to the Publisher, then the Publisher may at any time thereafter and at its option terminate this Agreement and return all rights to the Author by notice in writing and mailed to the Author's last known address.

4.   Production of the Work

The Publisher will publish the Work at its sole expense within a reasonable time after delivery of an acceptable manuscript and other required materials as outlined in Clause 3 of this Agreement. The manner and style of publication of the Work, including its price, format, manner of presentation and all other aspects of publishing, exercising or licensing to others the right to publish editions or versions of the Work and all subsidiary rights in the Work, will be determined by the Publisher. Printing plates, films, negatives, and any illustrative material commissioned by the Publisher will be the exclusive property of the Publisher.

The Author will proofread the galleys and page proofs and check the illustration proofs for accuracy. Alterations or additions (other than corrections of errors caused by the Publisher, the typesetters or the printers) may be made only with the permission of the Publisher. The cost of any such alterations or additions which exceed 10% of the cost of composition may be charged against the Author's royalty account.

Unless otherwise specified in this Agreement, the Author will deliver to the Publisher a manuscript for the index within two months following the receipt of page proofs.

5.   Royalty

a)   Definitions

Net Cash Receipts: Publisher's receipts from sales of the Work, excluding sales, value-added, and similar taxes.

Net Proceeds: Publisher's receipts from the sales excluding sales, value-added, and similar taxes, and production costs.

b)   Royalties

The Publisher will pay to the Author the following royalties:

  i)   Regular Sales

On each copy of the Work sold throughout the world through normal wholesale or retail channels except as otherwise provided in this clause: 15% of net cash receipts on the first 3,000 copies sold; 18% on all sold in excess of 3,000.

  ii)   Special Sales

On all copies sold at discounts which exceed the Publisher's wholesale discount schedules to customers whose normal business is other than wholesale or retail book distribution: 10% of Net Cash Receipts.

  iii)   Publisher's Special Editions

On all copies of editions, reprint versions or adaptations of the Work sold as limited special editions to other offices of the Publisher in developing countries: 10% of Net Proceeds.

c)   Other Rights

i)   Licensing

On the licensing of third parties to exercise any or all rights in the Work as described in Clause 2 of this Agreement (including, but not limited to, book club, translation or reprint licenses) the Publisher will pay to the Author: 50% of Net Proceeds.

ii)   Publisher's Exercise

Should the Publisher exercise any or all subsidiary rights in the Work as described in Clause 2 of this Agreement (other than in print or volume form) the Publisher will pay to the Author: 50% of Net Proceeds.

d)   No royalty will be paid on copies of the Work furnished gratis for review, advertising, promotion, bonus, examination or like purposes, or on copies returned to the Publisher unsold.

Should the Publisher at any time have damaged, unsold or returned copies of the Work on hand which are not salable on the usual terms, it may dispose of such copies; if such copies are sold at or below cost, no royalty shall be paid.

In the event the Author receives royalties on copies of the Work reported sold but subsequently returned, the Publisher may deduct such sums from any amount due to the Author thereafter. Accounting will be made annually in April for the preceding calendar year, and payments due the Author will be remitted at that time in US Dollars.

6.   Intra-Corporate Transactions

The Publisher will have the right to license any of the subsidiary rights enumerated in Clause 2 of this Agreement (including, but not limited to, translation or reprint licenses) to any of its subsidiaries, affiliates or divisions provided that the terms thereof are negotiated as a good faith transaction.

7.   Author's Discount

The Author will be given free of charge 6 (six) copies in total of the published Work and may purchase additional copies of the Work or other books published by the Publisher, but not for resale, at a discount of 33% from the list price.

8.   Updated or Revised Editions

Whenever the Publisher in good faith, determines that an updated or revised edition is desirable it will inform the Author and request the preparation of a manuscript for the updated or revised edition of the Work within a reasonable and agreed upon period of time. In the absence of a mutual agreement the period of time to negotiate terms will be ninety (90) days from the first notification of the Publisher. All royalties to the Author on subsequent editions will be computed according to the schedule set forth in the clause on Royalties as though it were a separate work.

Should the Author be deceased, unable or unwilling to prepare the manuscript for the updated or revised edition, the Publisher may make such alternative arrangements as it deems appropriate, subject to consultation with the Author (if available) concerning the possible selection of a revisor.

If persons other than the Author revise any editions of the Work, then the non-participating Author will receive as royalties on the first such revision fifty percent (50%) of the royalties otherwise due to the non-participating Author hereunder and twenty-five percent (25%) of such royalties on the second revision. For the third and any subsequent revised edition no royalties will be paid to the nonparticipating Author.

9.   Warranty

The Author warrants and represents that the Author is the author and sole proprietor of the Work; that the Author has not granted or assigned any rights in the Work to any other person or entity; that the Work is original to the Author; that the Work has not been published in whole or in substantial part by any other source; that the Work is copyrightable; that it does not infringe upon any copyright, trademark, or patent; that the Author has complied with Paragraph 3d) of this Agreement; that the Work does not invade the right of privacy or publicity of any person or entity; that it does not contain any libelous matter; that all statements that are asserted as facts are true or based upon reasonable research for accuracy and; that to the best of the Author's knowledge, no formula, procedure or prescription contained in the Work would cause injury if used or followed in accordance with the instructions and/or warnings contained in the Work. The Author will indemnify the Publisher against any costs, expenses, or damages including reasonable attorney's fees, which the Publisher may incur or for which the Publisher may become liable as a result of a breach of these warranties. These representations and warranties will survive the termination of this Agreement and may be extended to third parties by the Publisher.

10.   Competing Works

The Author will not during the continuance of this Agreement, without the written consent of the Publisher, publish any other edition or version of the Work, nor will the Author publish any other work which is, in the reasonable judgment of the Publisher, comparable to the Work in subject matter and scope which would substantially and adversely affect the sale of the Work. The Author may, however, after publication of the Work, draw on and refer to material contained in the Work in preparing articles for publication in scholarly and professional journals and papers for delivery at professional meetings. The Author will appropriately credit to the Publisher and the Work in any such use.

11.   Assignment

This Agreement will be binding upon and inure to the benefit of the heirs, executors, administrators, and assigns of the Author and the successors and assigns of the Publisher. By means of written instructions to the Publisher, the Author may assign any sums due hereunder now or in the future, but may not assign any obligations hereunder. The Publisher may assign this Agreement.

12.   Termination

If at any time the Publisher determines that the demand for the Work is insufficient to warrant its continued publication, the Publisher may declare the Work out of print. The Work will not be deemed out of print if it is on sale, offered by or available from the Publisher in any form permitted hereunder, or if it is under option or if any license granted by the Publisher is outstanding.

If the Publisher declares the Work out of print, then upon the Author's written demand, the rights granted by the Author under this Agreement will revert to the Author and this Agreement will terminate.

This Agreement may be terminated by mutual written consent. In addition, either party may terminate this Agreement if the other party commits a substantial breach of this Agreement and fails to remedy the breach within sixty (60) days after receipt of written notice sent by registered mail requesting remedy.

In the event of termination for whatever reason, all rights will revert to the Author, who will have the right within sixty (60) days of the date of termination to purchase any existing plates or negatives of the Work and original artwork and the Publisher's stock at cost. If the Author does not exercise such rights, the Publisher may dispose of such materials at its own discretion.

13.   Governing Law

Regardless of the place of its physical execution, this Agreement is being made under, and will be governed by, the laws of the State of New York without regard to its principles of conflict of law.

14.   Entire Agreement

This Agreement constitutes the whole understanding between the Author and the Publisher and no waiver or modification of this Agreement will be valid unless in writing and signed or initialed by both parties.

SIGN.   Author :.....   Date:......

Author's Citizenship:.....   Social Security Number:.....

XYZ, Inc. SIGN. Executive Editor   Date:....

XYZ, Inc. SIGN. President and C.E.O.   Date:.....

....

A careful reading of this document will show how much the dice is loaded in favor of the publisher.

Once the publisher received a completed manuscript— called a 'title' or 'project' in the book trade— it is assigned to a *copy editor*, the person who is in charge of the complex process of publishing. Designers will select the format, the typeface, the chapter and section headings and other attributes. A bad design can ruin a book on the marketplace. Editors and proofreaders will check and correct spelling and grammar, and suggest changes if they do not understand parts of the text. On some occasions they completely misunderstand a sentence and offer rewrites that make no sense. They also make sure that the material is *politically correct*. A 1997 edition of the author's *Hydraulics*[2] a historical footnote was included, pointing out that a certain significant mathematical concept "was invented by Pelagela Jakovlevna Polubarinova-Kochina, the only female among the major contributors to the field of hydrau-

---

2   Andrew L. Simon and Scott F. Korom: *Hydraulics 4e*, Englewood Cliffs, NJ: Prentice Hall, 1997.

lics." The footnote was pruned by a politically correct copy editor who probably considered it to be an insensitive fact.

Once the text was finalized, the work was sent to typesetters. Once typeset, usually a good six months after the initial submission, galley proofs were printed and sent to the author for review and corrections. Galleys are long metal trays holding the composed printing type. The galley proofs contain straight text, set into the width of the columns of the book in long strips of paper. This is the last chance for major revisions in the text. After the author's approval, page compositors put the text, illustrations and other components into pages. Page proofs sent to the author in batches, usually with a note of urgency. They were supposed to be checked for composition errors — mixed-up pictures, wrong captions, legends and the like. As soon as all page proofs were done, the pages were printed and photographed. The photographic negatives were prepared and the work was sent to the printers.

Big publishers have in-house printing presses, others, like university presses, use independent print shops. A lot of work is done abroad, Ireland, Singapore and elsewhere. The whole process, from submission to getting one's complimentary copies usually took 8 to 12 months. Most of America's $ 23 billion a year publishing business is still done this way.

When a publishing contract is signed, the author transfers the copyright to the publisher. The latter will have the right to make decisions concerning the size of the first print-run, whether there will be a second, third or forth edition, and so on. The publisher controls all matters of marketing and advertising, and also sets the list price of the book.

After a while, sales go down and the publishing house loses interest. There are new potential authors in the field, they must get their chances too. In the case of an apparently moribund book, the author may ask the publisher for a release. If received, the book may be taken to another publisher for a new printing. There are small publishing companies that specialize on such secondary work.

Electronic Printing

In traditional book publishing, before desktop publishing, electronic printing and print-on-demand came to life, the publishing company was in full control of the situation. It determined whether a manuscript will see the light of day. By and large, they controlled the content. Customers bought books for their content, not the container. In essence, in traditional book publishing, the maker of the bottle was in charge, not the winemaker. In the last decade of the twentieth century electrical engineers and solid-state physicists changed all that.

A manuscript produced on a personal computer could print out "camera-ready copy" that can be used for making the film negatives used by printers. The printing plates are made using the film negatives. It may also be 'print to disk' for the type of laser printer, or "imagesetter" used by the print shop. This made it possible to completely eliminate the function of the publishing house in the making of a book. By the end of the 1998, the 'computer to plate'

(CTP) technology was fully developed. It uses thermal imaging, rather than light imaging that involved a darkroom and the usual photographic process. The new $ 200,000 Creo Trendsetter machine, for instance, can transfer a computer text file directly onto a printing plate. Whether the text file was sent to the printer by a major publishing house or by a technologically savvy author is immaterial.

One remaining advantage of the big publishing houses is their ability to finance huge print runs for new books. The way printing contracts are usually written favors huge print runs. Print runs involving ten to twenty thousand copies are typical in the publishing industry. Anything smaller is called a "short run," with significantly higher per copy printing costs. A much advertised bestseller may call for an initial print run of 100,000 copies. An individual author can rarely finance more than a few thousand copies at a time. This way the marginal price of a single copy is significantly higher that if the print run would be, say, ten thousand copies. This relative disadvantage was wiped out by 'print-on-demand,' a new technology to be explored in the next chapter. However, one should recognize that there is an economy of scale in large print runs, and a book produced by print-on-demand is the least economical of all. But, regardless of the cost-differential, a book produced by print-on-demand (POD) would probably not be in print otherwise.

Incidentally, the cutoff is around 500 books. Using traditional printing technology for fewer than 500 books, a "short-run" is not economical. Printing more than that number at a time would probably call for traditional printing methods. (Assuming that the small publisher has money to be tied up in inventory.) In this instance, however, the so called "over/ under" unit cost — a printing jargon that would be called 'marginal cost' in economics— will induce the publisher to print more copies. "After all, they are so cheap." (But can you sell them?)

Toward the end of the 1990s, IBM developed a technology for high speed digital printing, at 130 pages a minute, with high quality print output. It allows the printing of a single copy of a book in less than five minutes, binding it and shipping each order within 24 hours. The new technology resulted in a number of alliances between IBM and large book store chains and wholesalers. Printing each book as the need arises enables booksellers to maintain smaller inventories, fewer warehouses. It also opens immense marketing opportunities for the one-person publishing house.

Lately, traditional printers, already heavy into computerized printing, offer print-on-demand services. Most have embraced electronic input, and switching to short runs presents no technical problems.

To assist a small publisher in locating a qualified printer nearby, there is a nationwide service organization:

Graphic Arts Information Network

Printing Industries of America

100 Daingerfield Road

Alexandria, VA 22314

www.gain.org

An excellent example of the modern book manufacturing process is shown on the website of Thomson-Shore, Inc., an independent, employee-owned firm. TS produces the books of many of the leading university presses of the country, as well as books produced by small publishers. Its address is

Thomson-Shore Inc.

7300 W. Joy Rd.

Dexter, MI 40930

www.thomsonshore.com

One interesting feature of the TS website is its virtual factory tour. It shows the book publishing process in a descriptive, step-by-step basis. It is quite educational for the novice publisher. Periodically, TS also offers seminars for publishers on new printing technology. Thomson-Shore is equipped with the most advanced computerized printing technology. Interestingly, they offer print-on-demand as well as drop ship service—direct delivery of copies to customers— in addition to traditional short run and full run printing.

An informative website for electronic color printing assistance is

FastColor.com

801 Commerce Street

Sinking Springs, PA 19608

This is actually a service bureau as well as an electronic color print shop. There are, of course, many others. Electronic color printing is still slow as well as expensive, but as color copier prices are falling dramatically it is expected to be economically feasible in the near future.

The nation's largest electronic printer is

Lightning Source Inc.

1246 Heil Quaker Blvd.

La Vergne, TN 37086

www.lightningsource.com

Lightning Source is a subsidiary of Ingram Book Company, one of the largest wholesalers of books. They not only print on an on-demand basis, but also offer assistance in selling the books, as Ingram supplies online and brick and mortar bookstores. A publisher could sign a contract for print-on-demand *and* short-run (minimum order 25) printing or for the latter only.

Ingram's major competitor, Baker & Taylor Books— a leading full-line distributor of books, videos, music and other information products— also has an electronic printing company called

Replica Books

1120 Route 22 East

Bridgewater, NJ 08807

www.replicabooks.com

established in 1997. Replica Books inventories its titles electronically, printing out copies of requested titles on-demand. Each finished "book block" is matched up with a newly printed, full-color laminated cover and bound in a library-quality hardcover binding. Replica accepts out-of-print titles at no cost to reprint under their own ISBN number in hard cover, offering a royalty. They advertise these books to libraries. Another choice offered by Replica is comparable to Lightning Source's contract for print-on-demand.

The rate of development and the growth of the print-on-demand business is staggering. By the end of 2001 Lightning Source Inc. established business relationships with over 1,300 publishers and printed over three million copies from a list of 100,000 digitized titles. At the beginning of 2002, Lightning Source and Baker & Taylor entered an alliance to market print-on-demand titles.

In one decade, the process of publishing has changed dramatically. No longer are writers subjected to the whims of publishers. Electronic printing provides an opportunity for everyone to bring his or her published product to a new, open market. A market that, only a few years ago, was entirely dominated by billion-dollar publishing giants.

There are a number of concepts that need to be learned before a person can embark on a publishing project independently. Basic requirements like ISBN numbers, copyrights, Library of Congress control numbers and other legal requirements must be known by a prospective publisher. He or she must also become familiar with the fundamental technical elements of book design, such as fonts, design and style. The hardware and software, elementary requirements for desktop publishing that are essential tools for preparing text for electronic printing should be acquired and their use must be learned. And then, there is the most critical knowledge: How to sell one's book on the bewilderingly complex marketplace.

In the past, these wide-ranging concepts were familiar to many different specialists from graphic artists, typesetters, compositors, copy editors, staff members of publishing companies. The prospective independent publisher must be familiar to some extent with all of these concepts. They will be presented in the following chapters.

At the end, methodologies are presented to unearth long out-of-print books that have not seen the light of day for generations. They number in the hundreds of thousands and many are not protected anymore by copyright. Most would sell quite well, if republished by an enterprising independent publisher.

Economics

In selecting a title for publication, a large publisher makes a costly investment decision. The expense of paying all the designers, graphic artists, proofreaders, copy editors, typesetters and compositors and carrying a big overhead for headquarters and a big sales organization had to be made up by the eventual profits on the sales of the book. Under the traditional system, all the author had to do was to provide a "publishable" manuscript. He did not have to worry about the design of the book, it has been done for him by the publisher. The author didn't have to advance a huge amount of money to pay for the initial print run, shipping, warehousing, advertising and distributing the book. With a publishing contract in hand, all the traditional author had to do was to send in the manuscript and review the galley proofs and page proofs several months later. Everything else was done by the publisher. Under this system, for every dollar of royalty that went to the author the publishing company pocketed about four dollars.

On the other side of the coin, not every book will make money. In fact, some knowledgeable publishers claim that only one in five books published in the traditional manner make a profit.

Traditionally, a publisher may order an initial run of, say, 4,000 copies of a book from a printer. In due time a truck with the 4,000 copies appear at the publisher's warehouse — or in front of the garage, in case of a small outfit. Ten cartons, each holding 20 copies, shrink-wrapped on a 40 by 48 inch wooden pallet, will hold, say, 200 books. The total shipment will contain twenty pallets. It will fill a one-car garage. It is a daunting sight. Along with this delivery arrives a bill from the printer, the cost of printing and shipping the books, to be paid in 30 days. For the 4,000 copies this could amount to $ 20,000 or so.

On the top of this investment, there will be additional expenses, such as advertising costs, warehousing costs, and order fulfillment expenses involving picking, packing, shipping, invoicing and collecting from the customers. On the top of this, there are the returns. Even with a very small operation, all this will require space and personnel. Experts suggest that a publisher must have at least a $ 2 million a year business to make this type of operation financially feasible.

Few of the roughly 4,000 small publishers in America make that kind of money. They must rely on help in the warehousing and order filling by contracting with larger publishers or by using fulfillment companies.

Big booksellers, like Barnes & Noble for example, maintain huge warehouses located strategically all over the country. They stock nearly one million titles for immediate delivery to either their numerous retail stores or their website. To establish a "warehouse relationship" with these companies a publisher starts by becoming a "vendor of record." All this requires is to fill out a questionnaire and provide a current list of titles. Once a publisher establishes this relationship, books will be ordered through purchase orders. Usually no more than two copies of each title will be held in a warehouse of a big bookstore chain. As the book becomes more popular, warehoused copies will increase. With no demand, some books may be returned to the publisher for a refund.

Fulfillment companies do not sell, all they do is to hold books in their warehouses for a fee and pick, pack and ship books on the publisher's request. They also handle the finances such as billing and collection. One example for such a firm is

Publishers Storage and Shipping Corporation

46 Development Rd.

Fitchburg, MA 01420

www.psscma.com

This company has warehouse facilities in Massachusetts, New Jersey and Michigan and serves about 250 small publishers.

Regardless whether a small publisher gets into the warehousing and fulfillment business or farms the job out for a fee, it is an expensive proposition. A rather large initial investment is at risk, and the potential for making a profit is far in the future.

Compare the described financial predicament to the case of a small publisher operating under the print-on-demand model. For a small fee, for example $ 50 to set up the cover and $100 for scanning in a 400 page book (25 cents per page), plus a yearly maintenance fee of $12, a major electronic printer will place the book in its computer. When an order comes, the printer will print a copy (or more, if desired), bind it and ship it to the customer within 48 hours. The per unit cost of printing is more expensive than printing thousands, but still reasonable, particularly since it is up to the publisher to set the list price. Shipping costs are on the top of this, but it is not any different than in the traditional method. All other aspects of the business is the same. The publisher still have to market the book and handle the accounting chores. But no huge up front investments and no warehousing, picking, packing, shipping, etc. are involved.

Today, the technologically competent author can decide to finish the manuscript on a word processor, design and format it with a publishing program like QuarkXpress or Ventura, convert it into some universally accepted format like Postscript or PDF file and send it to the electronic printer. In the case of the world's largest electronic printer, Lightning Source Inc., printing and distributing will be done by the latter, hence all the author has to do is to wait for the monthly check. It is not an exclusive contract, and the publisher is allowed to sell the books to others, paying printing and shipping/handling expenses. Replica Books Inc. works in a somewhat different manner. In their Standard Plan Replica furnishes the ISBN number, will hold exclusive rights, there is no setup or yearly maintenance fee involved, and Replica will advertise the book.

The distribution of revenue for a $ 25 "suggested retail" hardcover book, under the traditional system, was split as follows:[1]

Author: 10 percent

Publisher: 40 percent

Wholesaler: 20 percent

Retailer: 20 percent

Discount: 10 percent

POD technology has changed all this. When the whole-saler controls the printing process and the author/publisher pays for the printing and binding the income distribution might go the following way for the same $ 25 book:

Author/publisher: 25 percent

Printing (POD): 30 percent

Wholesaler: 25 percent

Retailer: 20 percent

To interpret these numbers one should consider that the typical print on demand contract, for example with Lightning Source, would require that the author/desktop publisher grants a 45 percent discount to the wholesaler and, in addition, agrees to pay for the printing cost. The latter is typically $5 for the hard cover, or $1 for paperback, plus

1   *Forbes*, August 21, 2000: Sources: Association of American Publishers; Anderson Consulting.

0.013 per page of the text. The wholesaler, who is now free of warehousing expenses (but had to invest in high speed electronic printing technology) will have to split the 45 percent discount with the retailer and the two together will have to absorb the cost of discount, if any. With increasing competition, the discounting of books are disappearing. Rather, for instance, Amazon.com has recently raised some book prices considerably over the list price, to maintain profitability.

Wholesalers' discount generally ranges between 55 and 25 percent. The former usually apply in case of cheaply produced books made for the mass market. POD titles are more expensive to produce, their discount is generally kept low. Who pays for shipping is also an important consideration. Wholesalers like to have the publisher pay for this, but in reality, the matter is often negotiable.

The print-on-demand contract with Lightning Source also allows for ordering either "short-runs," a minimum order of twenty-five books, or as few as a single copy, called a "drop ship" order. Drop shipping is a bit more expensive as an extra charge is made on a per copy basis, amounting to a dollar or so. This extra charge and the cost of shipping often exceed the printing cost of a copy. However, short run and drop shipping allows the publisher to sell books directly to other wholesalers, bookstores or individual buyers. Apart from printing and shipping/handling costs, sometimes there are no other expenses, like discount, involved.

There is a great deal of power in big-time advertising and general promotion of a book. Big publishing firms have a huge advantage over financially weak, small outfits in this aspect. Author tours for signing, advertisements, appearing on a TV show, interviews, reviews in newspapers and magazines or in the *New York Review of Books* on a Sunday boosts sales. But even with bestsellers, the shine will soon wear off. The publisher will decide to hand over the remaining copies to a "remainder firm" that sells them in bins in the alleys of drugstore chains. Within a year or two the book is out of print, the publishing company will be off to look for the latest to-be-bestsellers, and the author's name will soon be forgotten. We will revisit these topics later in the chapter on marketing.

Print-on-demand technology has done away with the concept of "out of print." Every year about 90,000 books go out of print in the United States. With print-on-demand this loss can be halted. Printing a single copy to fill an order from a bookstore, even ten years after the initial publication, will not be a problem. As long as the author/publisher pays a minuscule yearly fee, the book will remain in the memory of a computer, ready to be printed.

A typical, conventional press run for a book in America is 10,000. For technical and professional books it may be less than that. This, under the traditional system, puts great demand on warehousing, inventory and shipping. With POD the economics changes dramatically. The publisher will no longer need to print any more copies than what will actually be sold. In turn, the huge advantage of mega-publishing firms— those that put out the vast majority of the books published each year in the United States —will recede to a degree that will allow small publishers —indeed, some micro-publishers— to make some money without any significant initial investment and financial risk.

In addition to IBM, there are several companies building print-on-demand equipment. Sprout Inc. of Atlanta and Instabook Corporation of Gainesville are two examples. Getting the text file from memory or directly by the Internet, both can print and bind a book, for a single order, within a few minutes. The technical development of print-on-demand levels the playing field between major bookstore chains and small bookstores. When a large share of the books on the market will be digitized, any bookstore equipped with the technology will be able to offer just about any book for sale without investing huge amounts in warehousing.

Traditionally, a retailer orders the number of books it thinks it could sell. However, if the title proves to be in great demand, the store may not be able to satisfy it, because the wholesaler's inventory may be depleted. Alternately, small bookstores can not afford to keep slow moving titles in stock. This is when print-on-demand will be a big help. Another economic benefit is that small bookstores will not have to return books to the wholesaler they can not sell. In practice, this could amount to as much as one-third of the number of books initially ordered. Rather than ordering more than what they will ultimately sell, bookstores will not have to print a book until it is already sold.

In the future, e-book devices —portable book-size screens with a small memory and rudimentary operating controls — may download books from on-line bookstores or other sources. Some are already on the market. E-book texts are increasingly available for sale. While they have not yet gained wide popularity, in the near future another generation of e-book devices may potentially gain considerable market share. Eventually, e-books will compete directly with print-on-demand publishing. Whichever will prove to be more popular is not clear at this time. With the tremendous increase of memory capacities and decrease in size, it is easy to imagine a future when an e-book reader is equipped with a 10,000 volume library in a size of a matchbox. New text-display software and new kind of devices, such as tablet-sized PCs, will make onscreen reading, annotating and searching easier and more enjoyable than ever.

There are several companies offering their services in turning out reprints of long-gone titles with electronic technology. Some offer scanned copies of old books, long out-of-print, at highly respectable prices. A price of $ 99 for a single copy of a book is not unusual. Others are trying to lure academic authors of books on esoteric subjects, whose works were originally put out in very small numbers. Offering as much as 40 percent in royalties, these companies count on making money with high-prized books that are still protected by copyrights and are sold to a limited market.

Major publishing organizations have realized the importance of print-on-demand and e-book publishing and, for a while, made serious steps to capitalize on it. New companies were formed to accept manuscripts, offer full assistance in editing, designing, assigning ISBN numbers, registering with the Library of Congress —the whole works, except marketing and advertising. All the author had to do was to provide a manuscript and eventually market his book. But eventually the business model did not work out. One by one, the big firms, like AOL Time Warner and Random House, folded their e-book operations by the end of 2001.

Give onto Caesar

Operating a publishing empire from one's spare bedroom will invite, at one point, the scrutiny of federal, state and local authorities.

Selling books, like selling turnips, requires the payment of sales taxes in most states. As long as a publisher sells directly by mail order or by other, similar means may escape the attention of the state tax authorities. But once one starts selling to book wholesalers and bookstores, many will insist to follow the law and want to have a copy of an *Annual Resale Certificate* from Department of Taxation of the publisher's home state. To obtain this, one must register the 'publishing business,' pay a small fee, and receive a *Certificate of Registration,* that must be prominently displayed on the wall of the spare bedroom, or perhaps in the garage, right next to the pile of crates containing unsold books. Another necessary bit of inconvenience, particularly while the business brings in no income whatsoever, is the regular filing of quarterly state tax returns.

As long as one uses his or her own name for the business, or a recognizable variant of it, like John Smith Publications or Smith Publishing, there is no legal requirement that the business be incorporated. In case the business name is different from the owners name it must be registered as a fictitious name with the state's department of corporations. Once it is making money, incorporation may have some tax and other legal advantages. But at start, one's publishing business doesn't have to be a separate legal entity. This saves a lot of grief, particularly when it comes to federal taxation. Income and losses, including use of home for business, are to be reported on Schedule C of one's IRS 1040 tax return. For this, careful keeping of records is a must.

A corporation is a legal entity, created by state statue, with all the rights and privileges and responsibilities of a natural person; possessing the attributes of limited liability, centralized management, continuity of life and free transferability of interest. To form a corporation requires the filing of documents of incorporation with the Secretary of State's Division of Corporation. A modest fee is involved in all states. Supplies such as minute books, stock certificates and corporate seals are available at office supply stores. There are generally no laws requiring corporations to obtain any of these. Some financial institutions, however, require a corporate seal on documents signed by the corporation and are within their rights to do so.

There are various forms of corporations. The forms differ in the manner taxes are paid. Generally, corporations pay a state corporate income tax and assume liabilities. However, in the case of an S corporation the shareholders share income and expenses and report them on their individual income tax reports. It is advisable, even for owners of small publishing operations, to spend a few hours from time to time with expert professionals like accountants, financial advisors and attorneys. Selecting qualified professionals may be done on the advice of other small business owners, local Small Business Development Centers associated with some state universities, referral services and the local Chamber of Commerce.

Upon setting up a corporation, the Internal Revenue Service must be contacted in order to receive a Federal Employer Identification Number. This may be done by phone, calling 800 829-3676, or by mail, filing form SS-4. A quarterly federal tax and an annual unemployment tax return will have to be filed on behalf of the corporation.

Even if a publishing is operated as a sole proprietorship or partnership it must be registered with the state's tax authority. Soon after one receives the *Certificate of Registration* from the state taxation authority, the city, town or village authorities are notified. They get in the act by insisting that the 'publishing business' apply for an *Occupational License*, just like plumbers, flower shops and used book dealers. A yearly fee is charged for this license.

In most communities zoning and deed regulations do not allow the running of a business out of one's own home. The good news is, that in most places the town's zoning commission —in practice, actually a town clerk— will allow a publishing operation if it limits contacts with its clients to telephone and computer. By having a post office box for most business mail, this requirement is easy to satisfy. Nosey neighbors will have no opportunity to complain, as everything will be absolutely legal.

As soon as the publishing business generates money, it soon will become obvious that the finances of the business has to be separated from personal expenses. Most banks will not allow a deposit on an individual checking account if it is written for an entity like "Smith Publishing." A new business checking account will have to be opened. Most banks will insist that an Occupational License or Articles of Incorporation be shown before a business account be established.

ISBN

Who is a *publisher*, anyway? One could assert that a publisher is one who contracts with the author or the author's agent to arrange for a book's reviews, market analysis, design, editing, typesetting, printing, marketing and so forth. But when it comes right down to it, a publisher is one who has the right to assign an ISBN number to a book.

For a book the International Standard Book Number is like a licence plate to an automobile. ISBN was established in 1968 as an international standard numbering system for books and other monographic publications. The number is used to uniquely define a publication in accounting, ordering, stock control, sales data monitoring, and such other activities. In addition to being an order fulfillment tool, the ISBN is a bibliographic element in cataloging. It is used in bibliographic searches, printed on library cards, in catalogs and entered in national and international databases.

Today, the scope of the system has expanded to include other media such as calendars, spoken word audiocassettes, videocassettes and electronic media such as CD-ROM and DVD disks.

The International ISBN Agency is located in Berlin, Germany. Each country has its own agency to administer its ISBN program. The first few digits of the ISBN Number indicates the country where the number is issued. For example, The United States is either 0 or 1, France 2 and

Germany is 3. Some countries have as much as three digits. For example, Hungary is 963. Not all countries have their separate numbers, some are lumped into language groups.

The second group of numbers, after a dash, is the so called publisher's prefix, a number that identifies the publisher to whom the particular block of numbers was assigned. After the second dash, the next set contains the serial numbers of the titles, ranging from 0 to 9 (or 00 to 99, etc.). The last number, after a dash, is a computer generated dummy, which may be any number from zero to X. The latter stands for the Roman numeral 10.

In the United States, the ISBN duty is assigned by government contract to the R. R. Bowker Company, a division of Reed Elsevier, Inc., a venerable old publishing house. Anyone is entitled to apply for a series of numbers by contacting

ISBN Agency, R.R. Bowker

121 Chanlon Road

New Providence, NJ 07974

or call 877 310-7333 for application materials and information. Bowker's e-mail address is info@bowker.com. A would-be publisher can apply on-line. Information is provided on the R. R. Bowker web site:

www.bowker.com/standards/

In the application for an ISBN publisher prefix the applicant must provide a publishable address, the publishing firms name and any other imprints (alternate publisher definition), the name and address of the person submitting the application, the type of product (such as books, videocasettes, etc.) and the book subject area (such as history, law, sci-tech, etc.). Information on the number of books published or scheduled for publication and their bibliographic information, distribution arrangements with other entities is to be included also. For a one-time fee, which depends on the quantity of ISBN numbers requested (10, 100 or more), R.R. Bowker assigns a set of their ten digit numbers in a plain, computer print-out list. This apparently unassuming list should be carefully saved. There is a charge for its replacement by Bowker.

Fees in 2001 were as follows:

10 numbers - $ 205

100 numbers - $ 500

1,000 numbers - $ 750

10,000 numbers - $ 1,500

There are surcharges for priority processing and shipping.

It is wise to ask for a lot more numbers than one would initially expect to use. A block of 100 numbers would be a good size to start with. One could use up a lot, on account of the strict rules that must be followed. Some of these are as follows:

> There must be a separate number assigned for each separate binding for the same book: paperback, hard cover, library binding, and so on.

When a title is reprinted, the original ISBN number must be maintained, regardless of a price change.

A multi-volume work requires an ISBN number for the whole set, but if the volumes are sold separately, they need their own individual numbers.

Once assigned, an ISBN number can not be reassigned. These numbers can never be reused. However, the ISBN number is considered used only when the title is actually published. If not, the number assignment may be withdrawn and reassigned for a future project.

A revised edition requires a new ISBN number.

Ineligible for official ISBN listing are: Books with fewer than 49 pages, children's books, books on poetry or drama, bibliographies, and artists' books, Bibles and other standard religious books (Torah, Koran, etc.), periodicals and serials, audio-visual materials and other such items that may accompany books. While these will not be recognized as qualified books, they may have ISBN numbers assigned for purposes of billing and inventory control.

The ISBN number must be displayed in the 'verso' of a book—the page on the back of the title page   and on the back cover.

The ISBN number is valid only if all the ten digits are printed. Abbreviation is not allowed. For example: ISBN 0-9665734-9-X. (Note: Hyphenation varies with size of prefix.)

Using ISBN numbers is voluntary, like eating. No book-seller or distributor would deal with a publisher who doesn't use them. The Library of Congress requires an ISBN number before assigning a control number.

With the advent of the bar-code, the book trade introduced the so-called Bookland EAN bar code. This was devised by collaboration between the the International ISBN Agency, the Uniform Code Council (USS) and the International Article Numbering (EAN) System. The code provides for the ISBN to be printed in a worldwide compatible bar code format. The bar code shows the book's ISBN number, followed by the list price. It is usually printed on the back cover for easy scanning. There are several companies throughout the country specializing in supplying film masters for Bookland EAN bar codes. Stick-on labels with the same are also available. The cost of this service is quite negligible.

In addition to assigning ISBN numbers and maintaining an up-to-date list of all books on the market, R. R. Bowker publishes *Books in Print*, the hefty book familiar to most library visitors. Before the electronic revolution, this book, published once a year, was prominently placed at all libraries and bookstores. Today, R. R. Bowker supplies all libraries and bookstores with this information weekly by tape feed and on a CD-ROM disk that is updated every month. Bookstores search this source by ISBN number, author's name or title when ordering books. Other Bowker publications include *Children's Books in Print, Literary Marketplace, American Library Directory, American Book Trade Directory, Forthcoming Books, Ulrich's Periodical Directory*, and others.

Once a book is ready for publication, the publisher should assign an ISBN number to it by writing the book's title next to the number on the list. Once this is done, a Library of Congress Control Number (LCCN) should be obtained. This will be the subject of the next chapter. With the LCCN number at hand, the ISBN *Advance Book Information* (ABI) form should be filled out for the book. Blank forms may be obtained from the address below. (Bowker encourages photocopying the form.) This two-page form contains all necessary preliminary information about the book: Title and subtitle, the publisher's name and address, publication date, copyright date, number of pages, trim size, name of the author, the editor and other that of contributors, binding, projected list price, discounts, projected audience and so on. The completed form is to be sent to

R. R. Bowker Data Collection Center

P.O. Box 6000

Oldsmar, FL 34677-6800

The form may also be submitted electronically at the website:

www.bowker.com/titleforms/home/index.html

Once this information is filed, Bowker enters the data into their database.

It is advisable to keep a copy of the submitted Advance Book Information (ABI) form. Some of the data could change along the way. If some of the information changes, it should be communicated to Bowker. This, too can be done on the Bowker website:

www.bowker.com/corrections

under "Publishers, Distributors and Wholesalers."

In addition to its other duties, R. R. Bowker also administers the new Standard Address Number (SAN) program in the United States. SAN is a seven-digit identifier used to signify a specific address of a publishing organization or an establishment served by the publishing industry. This program was promulgated by the American National Standards Institute (ANSI) to be used to positively identify all buying and selling transactions within the publishing industry. SAN is required in all electronic data interchange communications using the EDI formats of the Book Industry Systems Advisory Board (BISAC). Major retailers, distributors and publishers all use this new system. To acquire a SAN number applications are to be made at

www.isbn.org

BISAC, by the way, is known for its extensive Subject Heading List which is used by major publishing organizations to classify books by their subject matter.

Library of Congress

United States federal law mandates that a copy of each and every publication must be deposited at the Library of Congress. The Cataloging in Publication (CIP) Division of the Library of Congress is responsible for assigning Library of Congress Control Numbers. Its mailing address is

Library of Congress

COLL/CIP (4320)

101 Independence Avenue, S.

Washington, D.C. 20450-4320

A Library of Congress control number is a unique identification number that the Library of Congress (LoC) assigns to the catalog record created for each book in its collections. Librarians use it to access the associated bibliographic record in the Library of Congress database and in other databases. The LoC assigns this number while the book is being cataloged. Under certain circumstances, however, a card number can be assigned before the book is published through the Preassigned Card Number Program (PCN).

Publishers residing in the United States are provided online means to obtain a Library of Congress Catalog Number before publication. For information and application, see

http://pcn.loc.gov/pcn

Completing an *Application to Participate* online —providing the publishing house's name, address, name of the principal officer and the name of the contact person and the list of imprints. Once a publisher's application is accepted, an account number and a password is assigned by the Division. There is only one account assigned to a publisher, unless, in the case of very large publishing houses, special arrangement is made. Saving the account number and password is very important. It must be furnished every time when the publisher applies for a Control Number for a new project. When a publisher submits a *Preassigned Control Number Application Form* for a new title, Library stuff make a decision as to its eligibility. The following are ineligible: Books which are already published, books which do not list a U. S. city as place of publication on the title page or copyright page, serials, government documents, items under 50 pages, (with an exception of genealogies and children's literature,) textbooks below college level, items not intended for wide distribution to libraries, religious instructional materials, expendable educational materials, translations except Spanish, mass market paperbacks, audiovisual materials, music scores and others.

Upon receiving the number, the publisher prints it on the back of the title page—also known as copyright page or verso—in the following manner:

Library of Congress Control Number: 2001119350

The number here is the control number of this volume. In previous years, during the twentieth century, the first two digits, like 98, referred to the year, followed by a dash and a six-digit number defining the book.

The Control Number is different from the copyright registration number. The latter will be discussed in the following section.

The Control Number must not be confused with the Call Number of a book in the Library of Congress. The latter is used to locate the book in the library. An example for the format of the Call Number is   CT954.S56 1998.

Searching the Library of Congress Catalog may be done on-line. The address is:

http://catalog.loc.gov

The catalog can be searched by author's name, title, etc. This site contains approximately 12 million records representing books, serials, computer files, manuscripts, cartographic materials, music, sound recordings, and visual materials. The catalog also displays searching aids for users, such as cross-references and scope notes.

For questions about searching the Library of Congress catalog, send an e-mail to:

lconline@loc.gov

Independent Publishing

52

Copyright

First-time authors usually show a great deal of concern whether sending their manuscript off for review is a safe thing to do. The common reaction to this by people of experience is to assure the budding author that everything will be just fine.

In 1918, Canadian writer Florence Deeks sent a hefty manuscript on world history to a well known publishing firm. Many months passed before the project was finally rejected and the well-thumbed manuscript was returned. Two years later, H. G. Wells published his well-regarded *The Outline of History*. Originally a scientist, Wells had no training in history whatsoever. He completed this two-volume panoramic work in 18 months, greatly adding to his literary celebrity. The similarity of the works by Deeks and Wells, in organization, structure, even turns of phrase, was striking. Eventually, Deeks sued Wells for plagiarism. The drawn-out case finally reached the Privy Council in London.[1] In one of his later works Wells wrote: "Fools make researches and wise men exploit them."

Novice authors should remember President Ronald Reagan's statement: "Trust but verify." Fortunately, govern-

---

1   See: McKillop, A. B.: *The Spinster and the Prophet*, Aurum Press, 496 pages.

ments protect the rights of individuals with copyright laws.

Copyright Laws

Copyright is a form of protection provided by the laws of the United States to the authors of "original works of authorship," including literary, dramatic, musical, artistic, and certain other intellectual works. This protection is available to both published and unpublished works.

Copyright is secured automatically when a work is created, and a work is "created" when it is fixed in a copy (or phono-record) the first time. "Copies" are material objects from which a work could be read or visually perceived either directly or with the aid of a machine or device, such as books, manuscripts, sheet music, film, videotape, or microfilm.

Copyright is a personal property right, and it is subject to the various state laws and regulations that govern the ownership, inheritance, or transfer of personal property as well as terms of contracts or conduct of business. It may be conveyed by operation of law and may be bequeathed by will or pass as personal property by the applicable laws of intestate succession. Any or all of the copyright owners exclusive rights or any subdivision of those rights may be transferred, but the transfer of exclusive rights is not valid unless the transfer is in writing and signed by the owner of the rights conveyed or such owner's duly authorized agent. Transfer of a right on a nonexclusive basis doesn't require a written agreement.

Congress adopted the first copyright law in 1790, establishing a 14 year copyright term "to promote the progress of science and useful arts by securing for limited times to authors and inventors the exclusive right to their respective writings and discoveries." Soon, in a political compromise, a one-time renewal for another 14 years was authorized. By 1909 the copyright term was doubled to 28 years, renewable for a second 28 years at the end of the first term.

In the Copyright Act of 1909 publication was a key to obtaining federal copyright on a work. This, however, is no longer true. The 1976 Copyright Act defines publication as follows: "Publication" is the distribution of copies (or phono-records) of a work to the public by sale or other transfer of ownership, or by rental, lease or lending. The offering to distribute copies (or phono-records) to a group of persons for purposes of further distribution, public performance, or public display constitutes publication. A public performance or display of a work does not, of itself, constitutes publication.

In the 1976 copyright law the term grew again: This time to the author's life plus 50 years, or, in the case of "works for hire," for 75 years. The 1976 Copyright Act generally gives the owner of the copyright the exclusive right to do and to authorize others to do the followings:

> To reproduce the work in copies;

> to prepare derivative works based upon the work;

> to distribute copies of the work to the public by sale or other transfer of ownership, or by rental, lease or lending;

to display the work publicly.

Before 1978, federal copyright was generally secured by the act of publication with notice of copyright, assuming compliance with all other relevant statutory conditions. The notice of copyright — that is, inserting the copyright, the date and the name of the holder into the work— was the responsibility of the copyright owner. It does not require advance permission from, or registration with, the U.S. Copyright Office. The notice should contain three basic elements:

> The symbol © (the letter C in a circle), or the word "Copyright", or the abbreviation "Copr."

> The year of first publication of the work.

> The name of the owner of the copyright, or an abbreviation by which the name is recognized. An example: copyright © 2000 Jane Doe.

Copyright notice in a publication was required before it was eliminated at the time when the United States adhered to the international Berne Convention, effective March 1, 1989. Essentially, use of the copyright notice may be important because it informs the public that the work is protected by copyright, identifies the copyright owner, and shows the year when it was first published.

Publications by the U.S. Government are not eligible for U.S. copyright protection. Copies of works published before March 1, 1989, that consist primarily of one or more works of the U.S. Government must have a notice and identifying statement excluding the copyright of the government's work, such as:

Copyright 1985 John Brown. Copyright claimed in Chapters 1 - 7, exclusive of U.S. Government tables and charts.

Titles published after March 1, 1989 do not require such statement. However, it is still wise to clarify this matter with appropriate wording.

Under the law in effect before 1978, copyright was secured on the date a title was published with a copyright notice, or the date of registration is the work was registered in an unpublished form. In either case, the copyright endured for the first 28 years from the date it was secured. During the last (28th) year of the first term, the copyright was eligible for renewal. The Copyright Act of 1976 extended the renewal term from 28 to 47 years for copyrights that were subsisting on January 1, 1978. In other words, a copyright that was renewed on or after 1950 is still under copyright protection. This means that books created as far back as 1922 are, potentially, not in the public domain.

The length of copyright protection of works created on or after January 1, 1978 is automatically protected for a term enduring for the author's life plus an additional 70 years after the author's death. In case of joint ownership, the term lasts until 70 years beyond the death of the surviving author.

Public Law 102-307, enacted on June 26, 1992, amended the 1976 Copyright Act to provide for automatic renewal of the term of copyrights secured between January 1,

1964, and December 31, 1977. This law also made renewal registration optional. Public Law 105-298, enacted on October 27, 1998, further extended the renewal term of the copyrights still subsisting on that date, providing for a renewal term of 67 years and a total term of 95 years.

The body of works unprotected by copyright and available for anyone to use or expand upon is called 'public domain.' The public domain contains all works for which the statutory copyright period has expired.For a publisher looking for a project, reprinting books that are in the public domain, —generally those published before the end of World War II and not renewed after the first 28 years— could be a legal and economically viable possibility.

It is illegal for anyone to violate any of the rights provided by the copyright law to the owner of the copyright. The unauthorized use of one's copyrighted work is called infringement. The test for infringement is whether an ordinary observer would believe one work was copied from another. "Fair use" of someone else's work is allowed under copyright laws. For instance, newsworthy or educational use is generally considered fair use. The factors whether a use is considered fair use or an infringement are:

> the purpose and the character of the use, including whether or not it is for profit,

> the character of the copyrighted work,

> how much of the total work is used and

> what effect the use will have on the market for or value of the work being copied.

In the event that a work is infringed, if a proper notice of the copyright appears on the published copy or copies to which the defendant in a copyright infringement suit had access, then no weight shall be given to such a defendant's interposition of a defense based on innocent infringement in mitigation of actual or statutory damages, except as provided in the copyright law (Section 504(c)(2)).

Usually, courts may decide that the damages for infringement of a copyright are the actual losses of the person infringed plus any profits of the infringer. In same cases, especially if the work's copyright was registered before the infringement, the court may simply award between $ 500 and $ 20,000 for each work infringed. If the infringement is willful, rather than accidental, the court can award as much as $ 100,000. To avoid such unpleasantness, using copyrighted material without the permission of the copyright owner must be avoided.

In practice, finding the owner of a copyrighted book might be extremely difficult, often impossible. In a later chapter a number of actual searches for missing authors are described. There are many potential scenarios for these occurrences. Sometime the heirs of a dead author disappear without a trace. Then again a book published over 75 years ago turn out to be still under copyright because the author was still alive when the "author's life plus 70 years" rule came into being in 1978. Many books are copyrighted under the name of a long-defunct company. It could turn out that there may be a "residuary trust" document hidden in the files of an attorney somewhere. Laws of many foreign countries claim that the ultimate heir of their citizens is the state. Does this mean that the copyright of a book written by a Soviet author before World War II and subsequently published in the United States is now owned by the government of Belarus or Russia or any other of the Commonwealth of Independent States?

The philosophical question may be raised whether a book of great educational and cultural value —out-of-print for many decades and totally inaccessible for today's readers— would or would not be allowed be salvaged by re-publishing even though nobody is around to authorize it.

It would be fair to assume that re-publishing an old, out-of-print book that may turn up to be still under copyright protection, in the definite absence of its owner, might be allowed under certain conditions, such as

> the unsuccessful search for the holder of the copyright is carefully documented,

> the original copyright statement is clearly shown in the new edition acknowledging its existence,

> a certain and customary amount is set aside from the book's income to cover royalties accruing the copyright owner once he or she may be identified,

> the book is removed from the market should the newly found owner demand it.

Copyright Office

The Copyright Office of the Library of Congress registers a copyright as a legal formality intended to make a public record of the basic facts of a particular copyright. Copyright, being a fundamental property right, does not depend on official registration. Registration is not a condition of copyright protection. But even tough it is not a requirement for protection, the copyright law provides several inducements or advantages to encourage copyright owners to make registration. Among these advantages are the following:

Registration establishes a public record of the copyright claim. Before an infringement suit may be filed in court, registration is necessary for works of U.S. origin. If made before or within five years of publication, registration will establish *prima facie* evidence in court of the validity of the copyright and of the facts stated in the certificate issued upon registration by the Copyright Office. If the registration is made within 3 months after publication of the work or prior to an infringement of the work, statutory damages and attorney's fees will be available to the copyright owner in court actions. Otherwise, only an award of actual damages and profits is available to the copyright owner. Registration allows the owner of the copyright to record registration with the U.S. Customs Service for protection against the importation of infringing copies.

Registration may be made at any time within the life of the copyright. Unlike the law before 1978, when the work has been registered in unpublished form, it is not necessary to make another registration when the work becomes published, although the copyright owner may register the published edition, if desired.

Information concerning the copyright status of a published work may be obtained from

Library of Congress

Copyright Office

Publications Section, LM-455

101 Independence Avenue, S.

Washington, D.C. 20559-6000

There is a fee (about $ 65 per hour) involved when a search is made on a particular title.

The staff of the Copyright Office answers questions concerning copyright registrations, and provides circulars. They are, however, aren't allowed to give legal advice. If information or guidance is needed on matters regarding ownership of a copyright, suits against possible infringers, the procedure of getting something published, or the method of obtaining royalty payments, it is advisable to consult a qualified attorney familiar with such matters.

Typography

Printing was invented by the Chinese about 200 AD. By 932 AD the entire classic Chinese literature was published in 130 volumes. In Japan, carving text in reverse into wooden blocks, inking them and printing on paper was well developed by 770 AD. Centuries after these oriental developments, mediaeval scribes were still painstakingly hand-writing illuminated holy books throughout Christendom.

About 1430 in Holland, metallographic printing— instead of using wooden blocks— was introduced. Brass or bronze dies of each of the letters of the alphabet were used to strike a text, letter by letter, into a soft layer of clay called matrix. Next, molten lead was poured over the clay to form a plate that showed the text in relief. That, in turn, was inked and used to print one page at a time.

In 1450, typography— that is making a die for each letter and casting many individual typefaces ahead of time from which to compose a text— was reputedly invented by the German silversmith Johannes Gutenberg (1398-1468) of Mainz. Having cases of typefaces at hand, the text for a line was set in a block. Consecutive lines of text were laid out and aligned to make up a page. Gutenberg also introduced the screw press for printing. He is credited with printing some 200 copies of the Bible. Each page had 42 lines and the whole work contained 1286 pages, published in two volumes. Most of the information about Gutenberg is second hand —from court documents about some inter-family litigation. Not a single book was found with his name on it. But Gutenberg's accomplishments in inventing movable typefaces, the printing press and the sheer magnitude of the work he has done —printing 257,200 pages for his Bibles— made him one of the greatest men of Western Civilization.

Printing with movable, reusable typefaces spread quickly all over Europe. For instance, in 1493, only 43 years after Gutenberg's invention, books were printed using Cyrillic typefaces at the Obod Monastery in Montenegro.

Fonts

The early Gothic-style typefaces used by Gutenberg, condensed, upright, almost void of curves, were quite difficult to read. Artists set out to design more readable typefaces. First, they followed the examples found on ancient Roman inscriptions. From these the Roman style —straight, vertical, upstanding capital letters were developed. From the letters in hand-written cursive Roman books of antiquity came the so-called 'lower case' style.

These typeface designs imitated letters in the hand-drawn mediaeval codices. The beginning of each letter showed the imprint of the scribe's pen as it first hit the paper. This characteristic mark, the short pen stroke at the end of lines, is called *sherif*. The typeface used in this text demonstrates this; for example see the top of the letters d, l, and k. It gave it's name to these types: sherif typefaces. Another characteristic of early typefaces was the *stress*, the gradual thickening or thinning of the line as the scribe increased the pressure on his writing instrument as he drew a downward line and released the stress as he turned around. The stress may be vertical or diagonal. Looking at the letter 'o' in this text shows vertical stress, as the top and bottom of the line thins out, imitating the trace as the scribe changes direction with his pen. Today's so called Garamond typeface style is a typical example of the so-called Old Style. They are still very much in use. This book is set in Garamond.

For the sake of consistency, designers developed a complete set of the alphabet, plus all other so-called characters, like # $ % ^ & * (+ { ! @ ~ ` < ? " ; ' / £ ¢ ¥ § and so on. In addition to these, special letters used in various non-English languages also had to be designed, in order to make the collection usable in all counties. Examples are: Ä å Ç é ñ Ö ü Ø ý Ă ĉ Ė ę ħ Ł ő Ŝ and many others. The accents on these letters are called diacritical marks. They give indications to the informed reader about how to pronounce the letter.

A complete set of the letters of the alphabet, capital and lower case numerals, punctuation and other characters together comprise a *font*. A family of fonts may include roman, italic, bold and extra bold, light and ultra light, extended and compressed and small capital — all designed in the same style. In some font families several hundreds of items may be found. Today's computer fonts often contain no more than 125 - 130 items.

The first successful font in the roman style was designed by Frenchman Nicholas Jenson in 1470. In the same time period, Italian Francesco Griffo designed a font with cursive Humanistic script, in which each letter leaned slightly forward. This new style became known as "italics." Alas, it is commonly pronounced eye-talic, that rhymes with eye-gnorant. Today, most font types are available in italics too. Here are a few examples: *This sentence is in Garamond italics.* **This sentence is in New Times Roman italics.**

In the 1600s, Holland became known for her outstanding typeface artists and printing technology. People from all over Europe went there to learn how to design typefaces and how to operate printing presses. After studying for a while under the renowned Dutch craftsman Dirk Vosgens between 1680 and 1689, Hungary's Nicholas Tótfalusi-Kis designed fonts that were successfully introduced in England, Germany and Italy. He also created fonts for the Greek, Hungarian, Hebrew, Armenian and Georgian languages. His fonts are still used occasionally in American book publishing under the name of Kis. This sentence is an example of the Kis font family. *This is in Kis italics.*

During the seventeenth century, English typography advanced greatly through the works of William Caslon, who, in 1722, designed the last version of the Old Style face which is still widely used. Another Englishman, John Baskerville introduced a modernized version, the so called Transitional design in 1740. It had greater contrasts between thin and thick lines in the typefaces and had a distinctly greater readability. His fonts are popular even today. The so-called Modern typefaces were introduced by Italy's Gianbattista Bodoni in 1788 and Frenchman Didot Firmin somewhat earlier. These Modern typefaces exhibited extreme contrasts between thin and thick parts of the letters and used very thin sherifs. Fonts named Caslon,

Baskerville and Bodoni are widely used to these days. This sentence is an example of the Baskerville typeface family.

During the twentieth century, modern artistic trends made major impacts in typeface design. One of the most significant introductions was the sans-sherif, (in French *sans* means 'without') and the uniform thickness in typefaces. The Gill Sans font designed by Eric Gill in 1928 is an example. **This sentence is set in a Gill Sans font.** Another very popular font of this genre is the widely popular Helvetica font. **This sentence is in Helvetica font.** Traditional designs did not go away, however. In 1932 Stanley Morison's New Times Roman font was introduced in the *Times* of London. Reminiscent of fonts used centuries ago, it is often used in American book and commercial publishing. **This sentence is set in Times Roman font.**

Today there are virtually hundreds of fonts available for the book designer. Computer programs for word processing and publishing come with several hundred fonts included. For practical considerations, however, a book designer rarely needs to have more than a dozen fonts to select a *body font* for text, another for footnotes, page numbers, etc.. Major titles and subtitles, index, legends and others may require other fonts. Most others will never be used, except perhaps for decorative purposes. Booting up a computer takes a lot longer when it has to load in dozens of font tables, hence keeping too many typefaces at hand is not advisable.

Size

Beside the shape and other design elements of fonts, size is another important matter. Typefaces are measured in *points* in American practice. There are about 72 points to an inch. Although the point system originated in France, European measurements are entirely different. Let's take a glance at how they came about.

Before the French Revolution in 1789, a national standard was established in France for measuring typefaces. The basic unit was the point, being 1/72 of a French inch. It was called Didot point,[1] after the famous typesetter Francois-Ambroise Didot. Printers in all countries liked the idea, they all adopted the 72 to an inch point system. The basic problem was that their standard inches were all different from each other. English inch was different from the American inch, German inch was different from the French one. In 1795 the metric system was made into law in France. As a result, France used two systems in typography. One was based the foot of an old king, another on the diameter of the earth. In 1879 the Germans adopted the Didot point system, altering it somewhat so that it became compatible with the metric system. But Americans and the British did not follow the German lead. In about 1887 they agreed to use the American inch as a base, and set a stan-

---

1   Actually, in France the point system was first recommended
     by Pierre Fournier le Jeune in 1737 but it wasn't widely
     adapted at the time. It called for 12 lines in an inch and 6
     points in a line. This is where the number 72 comes from.

dard point size as equal to 0.013838 American inch. This was slightly smaller than the European standard, and 72 points became fractionally smaller than an American inch: actually 0.996336 inch.

The particularly ludicrous aspect of this was that, according to U.S. law, the inch is strictly based on the metric system. The American inch is legally defined as 25.4 millimeters. The ultimate result of all this is that there is no agreement between Anglo-American and Continental printing standards. The difference is minute, but after a number of text lines it adds up and becomes quite noticeable.

The size of typefaces are defined in points. To understand this, a few geometric concepts must be understood.

> The imaginary line on which type is set is called the *baseline*.
>
> The height of small case letters such as x, m, s, a, etc. is called the *x height*.
>
> The extending part of letters like g, j, y, p is called the *descender*.
>
> The extending part of letters like k, h, t, b, is called *ascender*.
>
> The height of capital letters is called *Cap-height*.
>
> Finally, the distance — measured perpendicularly to the baseline — from the bottom of the descenders up to the top of the ascenders is the *point size* of a typeface.

Hence the easiest way to determine the point size is to add the heights of **b** and **p** and deduct from this sum the height of **x**.

It may be noted that the Cap-height is not necessarily the same as the point size. It is up to the designer of the font family. Furthermore, in some font families there are, in addition to the regular capitals, small case capital letters that are equal to the x height. These are called *small caps*.

In book publishing, most text bodies are set in font sizes ranging between 9 and 12. Footnotes, endnotes, index and so on could be as small as 8 points.

Depending on the font design, some typefaces, like Helvetica, for instance, have proportionally large x sizes, while others have relatively large ascenders and descenders. As a result, when two different fonts are set on the same page, one may appear to overwhelm the other, even though their point sizes are identical.

Line length of a text, such as in a columns, is also measured by points. One point is about 1/3 of a millimeter. It is called the *em*. One em equals the point size of the typeface used. By tradition, linear measurements sometime expressed in *pica*. One pica is 12 points, or 4.333 millimeters.

It follows, that an indent or outdent in a text is defined as one em or two em, and so on. The width of a column of text is also defined in ems. It should, of course, include the spaces between words. Research has shown that line length, that is, column width is an important part of readability. It is easier for the human eye, and mind, to quickly digest and understand text set in columns containing short —6 to 15 word— line lengths. Making column widths longer than that will decrease the readability of a text.

The distance between two successive lines of text — the vertical distance between adjacent baselines — is called *line feed*. It is often expressed in points. Numerically, 12/12, for instance, means 12 point font size with 12 point line feed. The second number stands for line feed. In this specific example, the descenders of the upper line of text (q, y, p, g) would just touch the ascenders of the lower line of text (t, f, h, k, l, b) if they happen to be vertically adjacent. This will not detract from the text's readability, because the case that two letters appear at the same vertical is rare. As long as the x height of the font is relatively small, there is quite adequate amount of white space between the lines to keep the text readable. In some cases line spacing of 12/11, or 9/8 is acceptable, particularly if the composition requires a lot of text to be squeezed into a small area. In books, on the other hand, wider spacing between lines is often preferable, particularly when the text column is long. Hence line feeds of 12/13, or 10/12 may be found in books.

Line feeds between paragraphs are another matter. In straight text, spacing between paragraphs could be as much as a whole empty line, to make each paragraph stand out. This, on the other hand, can not be done when, for example, a poem is quoted. In publishing programs this instance calls for an entirely new typographic setup, called tag,[2] using paragraph and line spacings that are equal, and often less than the line feed in the main body of the text.

This setting will keep the lines of the verse distinctly together.

Computer Fonts

In the early 1980s book writing got a boost by the development of word processing softwares. The early Scripsit program, sold for Radio-Shack's TRS-80 microcomputer (called 'trash eighty' by some at the time), was a very primitive product, but it freed the author from errors inserted by typists, and allowed unlimited 'cut and paste' manipulations of the text. Scripsit was followed by WordStar, a more versatile but just as confusing software, then Framework, which made possible the arrangement of the text in consecutive chapters. For PCs, an advanced word processing program called WordPerfect, than the Windows operating system, followed by Microsoft's Word brought word processing to new levels. They also put the venerable typewriter manufacturers out of business.

By the mid 1980s Xerox Corporation introduced Ventura Publisher. Ventura, even in its earlier versions, facilitated the design of a whole book, page by page, maintaining a uniform style: page size, typography, headers and footers, footnotes and endnotes, chapter and section headings, building of indexes, automatic page numbering and 'table of content' creation   the whole works. In effect, it replaced the work of book designers, illustrators and other

2   Tags will be described later in the Tooling Up chapter

artists, editors for spelling and grammar, typesetters and compositors. Desktop publishing was alive by 1990.

An early improvement of desktop publishing came about when Adobe Corporation introduced Postscript, the universal language of printing. Postscript is a page description language that was used to send instructions to a printing device on how to print a page. All the elements in a print job — including curves and straight lines of illustrations, and text— are represented by lines of Postscript code that the printing device uses to print a document. However, not every laser printer is Postscript ready, only the high-end ones, like commercial Xerox and DocuTech machines and the imagesetters used by printing companies. Application files, like Ventura, must be converted to Postscript files to print on these machines.

At first, Postscript used so called Type 1 typefaces. Later versions of Post Script typefaces, Type 2 and Type 3, introduced improvements that made it possible to print more complex graphics. Adobe offers an an immense variety of type-faces for digital work in Type 1 format. In addition to these, several companies market families of typefaces of great variety.

As a result, there is a tremendous selection of fonts available for personal computers. Many of them come bundled with word processor and publishing programs. In addition to these, there are several vendors, like Adobe, for instance, who offer families of fonts. Most of the fonts used in commercial printing are available for personal computers. There are three different types of computer fonts:

Printer fonts, that come with many laser printers, and used to be the only source for special fonts way back when the DOS operating system was dominant.

Post Script Type 1 fonts, offered by Adobe Corporation. It is a worldwide standard for digital type fonts.[3] A number of developers worldwide have created over 30,000 fonts in the original PostScript Type 1 format. PostScript 3 is now the worldwide printing and imaging language to communicate complex graphic printing instructions to digital printers. They are built into many laser printers for high-quality rendering of both raster and vector graphics.

True Type fonts, that come with the Windows operating system, were originally developed by Apple Computer and subsequently licensed to Microsoft. They have the advantage of appearing on the screen exactly the way they will print on a laser printer. In the early 1990s cross-platform incompatibility between Adobe Type 1 and Windows True Type fonts caused a lot of problems for designers and service bureaus.

Up until the early 1990s, computer manufacturers developed their own proprietary word processing programs that worked only on their own machines. A text document prepared on a Commodore or Radio-Shack machine was unreadable on an IBM PC or on an Apple. There was a plethora of mutually incompatible computer platforms

---

3   International Standards Organization outline font standard,
      ISO 9541.

and word processing and publishing software programs on the market.

In 1993, Adobe launched the Acrobat portable document file (PDF) format, which was a dramatic breakthrough in electronic document production. The introduction of PDF eliminated a lot of confusion. Adobe's Acrobat Reader program —a free download— when installed in any computer, allows the reading of PDF files regardless whether one uses a Mac or a PC, Windows or Unix. PDF encapsulates all formatting codes, fonts used, and so on. Another advantage is the relative smallness of the portable document file. A 250 page book, for instance, that takes up almost 3,000 megabytes of computer memory is compressed to 500 Mb in Acrobat format.

In 1996 Microsoft and Adobe has agreed to work out a joint specification for the next generation of computer fonts. The result of the agreement, after four years of work, was Adobe's release of eleven families of feature-rich Open Type fonts in the Summer of 2000. The new Open Type fonts work with Windows as well as with the Mac operating system. Open Type fonts can contain 65,000 plus multilingual characters, in contrast to the typical PostScript Type 1 font, that contains 228. Its other advantage is that its font files are significantly smaller than either True Type or Type 1 font files. Technically speaking, the Open Type is not an entirely new format. Instead, it is a hybrid, an extension of the True Type format that contains a "pocket" for PostScript font data, hence an Open Type font can contain either True Type or Type 1 font outlines.

The new Open Type fonts will mean a considerable advancement in digital typography. But for a while there will be a lot of older imagesetters around, therefore sending a manuscript in Open Style fonts to a printer without first asking about it may not be a good idea.

Design

Quality Control

In the big, traditional publishing houses a conceptual plan for a book is often nurtured by *development editor*s. They assist the author in transforming his or her idea into a book. Under their tutelage, the proper organization of the manuscript will take place early on. Even when a complete manuscript is submitted by an author it is reviewed by copy editors, spell checkers, fact finders, proofreaders and others to make sure that the final printed work measures up to the quality standards set by the publishing company. First and foremost, a *copy editor* makes sure that the book does not contain blaring spelling errors and embarrassing grammatical mistakes. He or she untangles questions whether *which* or *that* is the correct word in a sentence, and makes decisions on politically correct topics like when the word *black* should be replaced with *African-American*. Generally, a copy editor's job is to check the text for grammar, spelling, style and all-around appropriateness, making sure that the readers find the contents of the book smooth, readable and accurate.

Editorial standards are absolute necessities in the publishing world. They act as a unifying force, governing matters of taste and style. They provide consistency to a publication, the fundamental requirement for quality. In addition, they prevent possible legal action against the publisher by ensuring that the book does not violate copyright laws or does not defame someone.

Style guidelines allow editors to impose consistency by resolving questions that go beyond grammatical correctness. At their most mundane, for instance, these rules define whether one must use Arabic numerals or cardinal numbers to discuss quantities. Which is correct, *she ate 3 eggs* or *she ate three eggs*? A good copy editor would choose the latter, but the author can use either, as long as he or she is consistent throughout the manuscript. One does not need to create a style guide every time one begins writing a book. There are style manuals that have stood the test of time. These, and the whole matter of style, will be discussed in detail in the following chapter.

No writer or publisher can exist without a good, definitive dictionary. For $ 19.95 the *Merriam Webster Collegiate Dictionary* is a tremendous investment. A good synonym dictionary comes handy quite often, although both Microsoft Word and Corel WordPerfect wordprocessors have one built in.

Unless a desktop publisher has superb spelling, grammar, and editorial skills, it is advisable to hire a free-lance copy editor for a final review of a manuscript. The expense is a fine insurance against a potential major embarrassment. Copy editors use a set of traditional standardized markings to indicate what corrections are to be made in the text. For a good introduction to these marks, and copyediting in general Karen Judd's *Copyediting: A Practical Guide* is recommended.[1]

Fundamental Design Principles

Printing is communication, hence easy understanding of the message is essential. Grabbing the reader's attention with visual interest in the design of a page requires planning. One doesn't need a bachelor's degree in commercial art or industrial design to determine whether a printed page is visually appealing, boring, or downright ugly. But to explain why —and to know how to improve a page, if necessary— requires some basic understanding of the fundamental principles of applied graphic art. Application of these fundamental principles will make a page —and a whole book— easier to read and its message simpler to understand.

There are many books available on design. One that particularly stands out is *Looking Good in Print* by Roger C. Parker and Patrick Berry.[2] It contains numerous examples for good and bad design and is written specifically for desktop publishers. In the words of *The New York Times*: "If you can afford only one book on Desktop Publishing, this is the one."

Arranging text, titles, illustrations and legends on a page must be made with a purpose: To capture the readers' attention. One fundamental rule in page design is to have as

1   2nd Edition: 1992, 317 pages, Crisp Publications, $ 24.95, paperback.

2   Creative Professionals Press, 4th Edition $ 25.

much "white space" on it as possible. This requires grouping words, phrases and graphics in close *proximity*, forcing the reader's eyes to focus on them, leaving the rest of the page empty "white space." White space allows the eye to move and to rest. Used intelligently, white space can attract the reader's eye to certain portions of the page and ease the eye's movement from line to line. Related items should be grouped close together, clearly indicating that they belong together. Even with nothing else on a page but straight text, leaving too much space (leading) between lines conveys a feeling of shabby organization. Proximity is one of the fundamental principles of typographic design.

There should be no more than three or four individual element on each page. If there are more, the reader's eye will not focus on any but wander over them. Items will have to be grouped together into subsets to overcome this negative effect. Items shouldn't be stuck into corners or in the middle with equal amounts of white space between them. It causes confusion in the mind of the reader. In general, items should not be placed on the page arbitrarily. Each item must be in some kind of visual connection —*alignment*— with some other item on the page. One must identify a vertical or horizontal axis, or baseline, around which all items should be grouped. The beginner's conventional choice is to center all items on the page. This is a conservative, yet unimaginative design option. One should strive to avoid it.

By tradition, the first paragraph of the text is usually not indented. The purpose of this is to avoid the apparent misalignment between the title or subheading above this paragraph and the text block itself. Tiny misalignments like this add up to a thoroughly messy page. They obstruct the organization and prevent the unification of the page. Alignment is another one of the fundamental principles of typographic design.

Throughout a book, titles, subheadings, legends, tables and illustrations must be consistent in design and placement. To express this in other words, *repetition* is paramount. For example, once a typeface and a size for a title or subheading is set, the same setting should be repeated for all other titles and subheadings. Without such consistency, a book will appear to be poorly put together, will have a shoddy appearance. Repetition bestows organization to a book, an essential element of good communication. It also adds visual interest to each page. Fortunately, the integral principle of all publishing software, tagging, assures such consistency. Repetition is an additional fundamental principle of typographic design.

To enhance visual interest, various elements or items in the design should contain repetitive differences. Such contrasts are extremely effective in organizing the information presented. When two items are primarily different, like body text and subheading text, their contrast must be very striking. *Contrast* is really effective if it is strong. To be strong, it must create a contrast between the two items. If the difference is only slight, it will create *conflict*, rather than contrast. Conflict is disharmonious, it must be avoided. Similar typefaces, like ones from the same type family, are *concordant*. They make the page appear harmonious to the point of dullness and boredom. For instance, if one uses 12 point **Times** font for body text, for subtitles one shouldn't select a larger font from the same typographical family. Selecting a 14 point **Helvetica**, or a cursive type like *Vladimir Script* to ensure the necessary contrast. Without such drastic difference, the contrast will not be effective. It will not attract the reader's attention. Contrast is the fourth fundamental principle of typographic design.

To repeat, the essence of all of these: proximity, alignment, repetition and contrast are the four basic principles of design.

Color

In designing book covers and dust jackets, even inserting an occasional colored illustration, desktop publishers must be familiar with the basic concepts of color. Definition of colors in the printing business is drastically different from those in computer technology. The publisher must be familiar with both systems.

Before color printing, most illustrations were black and white halftones or bitmaps. Halftoning is a process of breaking a gray image up into groups of black spots. Black or white only can be described as one bit color mode: either black or white. To produce halftone spots the computer groups several adjacent pixels into a group, and to define a gray it turns on or off some of the pixels within the group. Black and white combined in various proportions yields Duotone and Grayscale models. Experts claim that the human eye can discriminate between 256 shades of gray. Commercial imagesetters can create dots as small as 2,400 - 3,000 dots per inch, often too small for the human eye to see. Essentially, an imagesetter is nothing more than a film-output device that transforms an electronic text file of a page into a film negative, which, in turn, is used to make press-ready printing plates. It may sound simple, but imagesetters sell for about $ 300,000.

Color can be defined by various means, called models. In one model, color is defined by its hue, its saturation and its brightness. *Hue* can be expressed by a rotational angle on a color wheel. *Saturation*, the vividness of color, and *Brightness*, the amount of white in the color both can be expressed as percentages. Using these three variables is the HSB model of color definition.

The human eye sees 'color' when light waves pass through or are reflected by objects. In essence, colors of light are various wavelengths of electromagnetic radiation. In the visible range, the longest wavelength is red, the shortest is blue. Green is about halfway between them. These three are called primary colors. Any color con be defined by mixing the three primary colors in various percentages. This gives rise to the RGB model of color definition.

Television screens and computer monitors are cathode ray tubes made up by an array of dots, called pixels, containing electro-luminescent minerals (phosphors containing small amounts of activators of various kinds) that emit the three primary colors (Red, Green, and Blue) when electronically excited. At each tiny dots there are three emitters, one for each color. They are so close tor each other that human eye blends them together, seeing their combined color.

In the digital world, information is transmitted in binary units, *bits*: On or off, one or zero. In the digital world the base of eight is used to convey information, rather than the common base of ten in the decimal system. This is so because the number eight is successively divisible by two, always resulting in a whole number (4, 2, 1, contrary to the decimal system that results in 2.5 after the second division.) Seven data bits and one stop bit makes up a *byte*. Each color value is described by a byte. In the RGB system there are three color values, one for each of the three color emitters, or channels, at each pixel. Three bytes, eight bits each, combine into 24 bits of data.

Adding together the three primary colors at various intensities produces the range of colors one sees on the monitor screen. The intensities range from 0 to 255, a total of 256 possibilities. As each of the three color channels have 256 possibilities, the three combined allows the description of $256 \times 256 \times 256 = 16,777,216$ different possible color values in the RGB model.

Intensity could also be expressed in a percentage, ranging from one to 100. Emitting 100 percent of each of the three colors results in pure white pixel on the screen. When the intensity of each is equal, the result is a shade of gray. This RGB color model is the default in graphic software programs. To see the right colors on the monitor, the program must be set to RGB.

Printers use translucent inks to create full color. As white light strikes these inks, part of the light waves are absorbed, another part is reflected back to our eyes. Theoretically, equal amounts of pure cyan, magenta, and yellow paint pigments should combine to absorb all color and produce black. But printers inks are never pure, therefore their equal mix results in a muddy brown. Black ink must be added to produce true black color. Hence this color model is called CMYK, in which K stand for blacK, to prevent confusion with blue. In a print shop, color processing requires the separation of each color, as the printing machine can print one colored ink at a time. It is called *four-color process printing*.

Printers should receive electronic files for color copy in CMYK model. If, by mistake, the file is set to RGB, the final outcome will be significantly different from what was expected.

Modern four-color printing presses are able to print at 1,200 dots per inch or more, imperceptible to the human eye. This makes it possible to apply each of the four colors on small areas in various degrees of intensity. Before printing, the four colors are segregated and the four color files are placed on film negatives called color separations. These separations are used to burn plates to be used in the offset lithography printing process.

For each dot on a printed paper there are four color channels, one for each of the four process colors. Expressing this concept digitally, there are 4 times 8 bits, or a total of 32 bits describing the combined color value at each dot in the CMYK model. With a bit depth of 32 bits (4x8), means that CMYK can produce 4 billion colors.

Each electronic device, such as a monitor, a scanner or a color printer has a range of colors it can handle. This is referred to as the *color gamut* of the device. Even ink on paper has a color gamut. Due to the difference in color gamuts of scanners, monitors, etc., one can not rely on the monitor for accurate color. There are color management systems available for calibration, but they need to have a closed loop system to properly calibrate. The process is to scan an image, output it to an imagesetter, print it on the press then using the calibration utilities set up the monitor to match the printed piece. Once any variation is made on the system, such as using a different scanner, the whole process must be repeated.

Color separation and four-color process printing are not required if only a single, pre-mixed color is used, such as in the case of a logo on a business card. Such single application is called *spot color*. The designer select a color from the industry-standard *Pantone Matching System*, that included in swatch-books and chip-sets. Using this system, one can select, for instance, the Pantone® 274CV for a particular shade of blue desired. The print shop then makes the required ink by combining carefully measured amounts of two or three inks from a set of 14 primary colors, plus white. Originally, 500 specified spot colors were mixed from just eight basic inks, plus black. Later the number of spot colors were gradually increased. By the year 2001, Pantone increased this number to 1,114. The latest swatch books are printed not only on white paper but on matte-coated, coated and uncoated papers. Pantone colors aren't only used in printing. They set the standard to textile and furniture design, as well as in e-commerce.

As mentioned earlier, printers insist to receive color work in CMYK model. Since the designer uses the RGB model, conversion is necessary. While theoretically this is possible, there are some potential practical difficulties. Monitors rarely produce the exact color as set in the program, even if the monitor was carefully calibrated. Subtle effects such as ambient lighting, the age of the monitor, design done during the monitor's warm up period can combine to set the designed colors off. Viewing the design on another computer monitor could result in marked differences in colors. RGB values could change slightly from system to system using different monitors. After the material is printed, the designer can face an unpleasant surprise.

Device-independent color matching systems can overcome the differences. Usually a swatchbook is used as a reference for selecting the desired colors. One such widely accepted standard is the Pantone® Matching System, discussed earlier. Another device-independent matching system is the CIE Lab[3], promulgated by an international standards commission in 1931, the *Commission Internationale de l'Eclairage*. This color model is based on human color perception. It is based on lightness value L (white $= 100$), and two chromaticity ranges: green to red (a) and blue to yellow (b), hence Lab.

The larger the mode —such as 32 bits versus 8 bits of information for each pixel— the larger the file will be that contains the work. For this reason, color design files tend to be huge, even in compressed format. The designer must keep this aspect in mind when selecting a color model and picking the file format to save it.

---

3   Sometimes written as CIE L*a*b.

The most accepted file format to submit color work is Tagged Image File Format or TIFF. This was specifically developed for page layout applications and is supported by all image editing platforms. Another advantage is that it is platform-independent. It can be made on a PC and can be viewed on a Macintosh or vice versa. TIF files [4] can save RGB, CMYK and CIE Lab color information.

For instance, to design a book jacket in full color, one needs to provide three TIF files, front, spine, and back.Each is sized to fit the book plus a small extra margins all around, called *bleed*, to allow for trimming. (On the bottom right hand corner the book's ISBN number must be shown.)

In case of a dust jacket, five TIF files are to be supplied to the printer: front, spine, back and the two flaps, one for the front and one for the back. The width of the flyleaf varies, usually it is wide enough to hold about 2.5 inches of text. Like for the cover pages, all five should be sized to allow for at least 1/8 inch of bleed.

Spine Width

As an afterthought, we should mention an important element of book cover design, the width of the spine. The

---

4   The second F is commonly omitted.

spine width, or bulk, is designed with the number of pages of the book in mind. The formula for this is:

$$W = 2 \times A + B \times P/2$$

Where W is the width of the spine,
A is the thickness of the cover page,
B is the thickness of the paper stock used, and
P is the number of pages in the book.

For a customary 60 lb. offset paper and the common paperback cover stock this formula would result in

$$W = 0.02 + 0.0023 \times P$$

At least 1/8 of an inch bleed should be added to this, all around.

Independent Publishing

90

Style

Most publishing houses hire copy editors to make sure that manuscripts are free of errors and follow the established style of the house. Some newspapers and magazines develop style books, that cover every conceivable situation. One example, for instance, is the 154 page *The Economist Style Guide,*[1] published by the venerable British magazine. *The Economist* was first published in 1843, so they must have gotten their style down right by now. The latest edition of this best-selling guide, published in 2000, is based on the magazine's own house style manual, and it is an invaluable companion for everyone who wants to communicate with clarity, style and precision for which *The Economist* is renowned. The book gives general advice on writing, points out common errors and clichés, offers guidance on consistent use of punctuation, abbreviations and capital letters, and contains an exhaustive range of reference material — covering everything from accountancy and stock market indices to laws of nature, science and economics. Also included is a special section of the differences between British English and American English.

The classic book on this subject, now in its fourteenth edition, is *The Chicago Manual of Style: The Essential Guide for Writers, Editors, and Publishers.* It is widely available for $ 45.

---

1   This hard cover book is available online for about $ 25 at www.economist.com

It now covers the whole publishing business, even provides information to desktop publishers about how to get an ISBN number and what are the basic design requirements for a dust jacket.

Another standard text on writing style is *The Elements of Style* by William Strunk Jr. and E. B. White ($ 14.60 in hardback and $ 5.56 in paperback). Reviewing it, *The New York Times* wrote: "Buy it, study it, enjoy it. It is as timeless as a book can be in our age of volubility." Both of these texts are widely used in academia for theses and dissertations, as well as in the printing world. Strunk's *Elements of Style* can also be found online, at

www.bartleby.com/141/index.html

Additionally, a very useful general online reference source is the Internet Public Library Reference Center:

www.ipl.org/ref/

Copy editors for most major publishers develop a style sheet for each book *after* the author submits a manuscript. Such style sheet combines general recommendations with peculiarities of the particular book. The latter, for instance, codify such oddities like the word *gage* for water level measuring in hydraulic engineering, when the correct spelling in other fields would be *gauge.*

One example for a style sheet, developed at one time by an overeager copy editor, is shown below:

"Here are some common errors:

NUMBERS: Uniformity is important. One convention is to spell out numbers through twelve, then use Arabic numerals beginning with 13.

Convert the word "thousand" to the digits "000" where appropriate, which is almost everywhere. You can follow the lead of quotations you use; one of them spells out "eighteenth," "nineteenth," and "twentieth" century.

QUOTATIONS: Your quoted sources are barely distinguishable from your own text. Indentation and smaller type are needed.

In multi-paragraph quotations, only the last paragraph should end with quotation marks. The earlier quoted paragraphs begin with quotation marks, but should end without them.

The first time you quote a person, it is important to identify him; thereafter you need not (although you might allude to your earlier quotation from the person).

The quotation mark belongs after the comma or period, not before it.

In quotations from other sources, italics must appear in the source quoted. If they were added for emphasis; it must be so stated, to avoid misrepresenting the source quoted.

Quotations must be copied exactly; if the source quoted contains an error, put a note after the error in parenthesis, to show that you caught it.

QUOTATION MARKS: Single and double quotes are not interchangeable. Use double quotation marks routinely; only if another quotation appears within a quotation does it become necessary to differentiate it, which one does by using single quotation marks.

CAPITALIZATION: Nouns are routinely capitalized in German, but not in English. Unless you are referring to a particular university or professor, the word is lower case. Sophomore, junior, and other quasi-titles also are lower case.

PUNCTUATION:

PERIODS: Put two spaces after each period that ends a sentence. Otherwise, ideas run together and confusion results.

HYPHENS: Remove the hyphens from "high school" and "liberal arts," especially where you use the terms as nouns! When you use them as adjectives, hyphens are unnecessary and could irritate the reader.

DASHES — Insert a space before — and a space after.

ACUTE ACCENTS: If you are going to use the French acute accent, use it throughout.

SUPERSCRIPTS: The place to put your numeric superscript to indicate a footnote is at the end of the quote.

NOT SYNONYMS: "Economic" and "economical" are not interchangeable; ditto "institute" and "institution," "victims" and "victimologists," and "education" and "educational."

ABBREVIATIONS: The first time you use an abbreviation, write out the term, followed by the abbreviation in parentheses; thereafter, you can use just the abbreviation. For example, the first time write "Massachusetts Institute of Technology (MIT);" thereafter, "MIT" will suffice.

NOUNS AND VERBS SHOULD AGREE: Singular nouns require singular verbs; plural nouns require plural verbs; ignore the prepositional phrase; for example, "the total number of colleges is," not "the total number of colleges are."

An author does not necessarily have to comply with all recommendations made by the copy editor. In the list shown
above, there are a few recommendations that go against
rules used by major publishers. Often the copy editor completely misunderstands the author's meaning, in which
case explanations are necessary and an appropriate change
in the text is recommended. More contentious differences
may occur if the copy editor insists on making deletions or
changes based on differences of ideology.

Refining a manuscript to agree with all possible grammatical and stylist rules is arduous. When trying to be perfect,
there is also the possibility of reaching the point of dimin-
ishing returns — which you can recognize only by passing
it.

Independent Publishing

96

Equipment

Users of the leading wordprocessor programs, mainly Microsoft Word® and Corel WordPerfect®, often argue that their programs have all the necessary features to make consistently formatted long documents, like books. These claims are erroneous. Professional publishing programs' formatting capabilities far exceed that of any word processing software.

As introduced earlier, designing a book involves the individual design of each typical paragraph, including titles of various levels (chapter, section, etc.), footnotes, endnotes, page numbering, index and table of contents. Typefaces, type sizes and spacing used in every one of them should be defined. In electronic publishing, the sum of all of these details constitute tags. Once a text is imported or typed into a document, each element is tagged. This is the essence of publishing programs. Tagging each element of the book allows the designer to make consistent changes in the whole body of the book by making a change at one point only that is automatically carried over to all similar tags. The result is a consistent design of the whole book, from beginning to end.

Tags encapsulate the design of a paragraph, typeface, font size, spaces above and below, and other characteristics. There are tags for chapter titles, section titles, captions for figures and tables, bulleted lists (even if there are no bullets) etc.. One can see the need, for example, for a special tag for a bulleted list of items, that otherwise, using regular body tags, would be spread out on the paper because of the paragraph leading after each item. The same situation applies when a postal address, or an Internet website address, is included into the body of the text. Tags allow consistency in a book which would be hard to attain otherwise.

Word processing programs do apply some tagging, mainly chapter and section title designs, but not nearly to the extent used in publishing programs. Word processing software usually allows the selection of typefaces and font sizes. Publishing programs do the same, but can vary the space above and below the lines, and above and below paragraphs. Also, for instance, word processors usually use the same typeface in footnotes that is used in the main text. Publishing programs have an almost infinite variety to manipulate text and graphics on a page.

There are other unique capabilities of publishing programs. Key words, for instance, can be included in an index. Subsequent changes and rearrangement in the chapters, sections or other parts of the book around will not affect the index: Once set up, page references in it are changed automatically, as they are encapsulated in the text.

Historically, Apple was the first to hit the market with book formatting programs. The initial advantage of Apple's QuarkXpress® publishing program stemmed from the fundamental graphic user interface (GUI) design used by Apple. The DOS based IBM PC system took years to ketch up with Apple in this regard. Today, QuarkXpress is available both for Mac and Windows. Adobe Corporation, known for its awesome collection of typefaces and its Acrobat cross-platform portable document format, promotes its PageMaker® (originally Aldus PageMaker) program. It is fully integrated with the Adobe Illustrator ® and Adobe PhotoShop ® programs. PageMaker is excellent for creating complex, artistic color pages commonly found in glossy magazines. The latest Adobe program to enter the market, In Design ® offers even greater capabilities for manipulating text and graphics. Microsoft competes with these programs with its Publisher ® program and others.

In the mid 1980's, Xerox Corporation made big strides in developing Xerox Ventura Publisher for the IBM PC system. It is particularly useful for creating long, multi-chapter books. Today, owned by Corel Corporation, Ventura ® 8, the latest version and its next generation is being tested in beta form. Corel DRAW ® and Corel Photo-Paint ® are the graphic programs integrated with WordPerfect and Ventura.

Every one of these programs have full capabilities to use hundreds of typefaces, adjust the size and spacing of letters, lines and paragraphs, apply consistent rules for every possible aspects of typesetting. All of these major publishing programs have their comparative advantages and disadvantages. They have their detractors and enthusiasts. Those who are familiar with all, generally agree that in situations requiring elaborate page designs and lots of graphic elements QuarkXpress and Adobe PageMaker are preferred over Ventura. On the other hand, for long documents such as books, with relatively few tables and illustrations, Ventura is preferable.

While for most books graphic design capability is rarely used, all publishers need at least one graphics program. Any scanned illustration, even the simplest drawing or a photograph downloaded from the Internet need to be converted into a graphics format using Corel Photo-Paint or Adobe PhotoShop or another such program to be imported into a desktop publishing project. Fortunately, makers of publishing programs recognize this need. Often, as in the case of Corel Ventura, the associated graphics program, in this case Photo-Paint, is sold bundled together.

Another aspect of the selection of one's first publishing program is the word processor software one favors. Users of Microsoft Word will find that Microsoft's Publisher is fully integrated with their word processing software. Corel Ventura, on the other hand, is fully integrated with WordPerfect—another Corel product. In practice, these relative advantages are not all that important. Ventura will import Word files just as well as it does WordPerfect files. In the rare occasions when direct import is not possible, the file may be first converted into RichText format, for instance, which will import at ease.

A minor advantage of WordPerfect involves accented characters of foreign languages, like ö, ú, ô, ÿ, and ş. Microsoft Word does have some limitations in this area. There are a few letters is some foreign languages that Word can't reproduce correctly, while WordPerfect will have no such difficulties.

Publishing programs have full word processor capabilities, including spelling check and hyphenation facilities. Some

facilities —like table formatting, in the case of Ventura —
are inferior when compared to word processor programs.
Importing word processor files—including tables, in this
instance—is the favored method. In the case of
multi-chaptered books, for example, importing the text
chapter by chapter is highly preferable.

One of the importance of importing text and graphics in
small portions —chapters, for instance— is the possibility
of corrupted files turning up. It is an unwelcome occur-
rence during processing when the screen freezes up, and
the message

*"This Program Performed an Illegal Operation and Will Be Shut Down.
If This Problem Persists, Contact the Program Vendor."*

Almost always,the problem is caused by an imported file
that is somehow corrupted. Finding the source of corrup-
tion is often impossible. Frequently the only solution is to
delete the bad file and import the text again, after careful
checking for possible errors in it in the original word processor file. A footnote erroneously labeled as endnote
could cause a problem, for instance, bringing about weird
things, like, for example, miraculously appearing repeated
phrases at the end of a footnote. Other potential problems
may be caused by formatted tables in the original document. It is best to cut them out and save them elsewhere,
moving them into the text once the rest of the file is safely
installed.

Reference to the possibility of a "Corrupted File" appears
in software literature about as often as a social reference in
Victorian society to a hydrocephalic relative who is kept in

a closet. But in real life they do occur. The solution is the drastic use of the delete command. This, incidentally, points to the necessity to save one's work in an archival file: Original scans, wordprocessor files and so on. Frequent saving and backup are strongly recommended.

Hardware selection for publishing programs is no more involved than that for common word processing software. Any ordinary computer will be able to handle the job, particularly if the project is not laden with graphics. A typical 250 page book with plain text can be transferred to a 1.2 Mb capacity 3.5 in. floppy disk. Printers usually require that manuscripts be submitted on CD-R or on a 100 Mb or larger capacity Iomega Zip disk. Both have a storage capacity to hold many books. The former happens to be a very cheap medium.

Hardware needs for graphics programs are much more stringent than for word processing or publishing needs. A graphics file for a color cover page can be as big as 20 megabytes or more. Unless one has a fast microprocessor and plenty of RAM, file handling can be agonizingly slow.

Previously typed or printed text may be imported through a scanner. Scanners are not expensive but one has to be selective when buying them. Some scanners on the market are not quite satisfactory. Scanner quality is defined by the degree of resolution.

Although the concept can be confusing, scanner resolution is just a measurement of how many pixels a scanner can sample in a given image. An acceptable scanner should sample a grid of 300 x 300 pixels for every square inch of the image. It sends a total of 90,000 readings per square inch to the computer. Higher resolution scanners cost more and produce better results. A scanner with a 600 pixel/inch resolution gives very satisfactory results. There are some scanners on the home office market that are said to scan at 1,200 pixels per inch.

Unfortunately, things are not that straightforward in the real world. There are actually two ways of measuring resolution, and manufacturers occasionally obscure them in the hope of selling more of their products.

Optical Resolution: A scanner's optical resolution is determined by how many pixels it can actually see. For example, a typical flatbed scanner will use a scanning head with 300 sensors per inch, so it can sample 300 dots per inch (dpi) in one direction. To scan in the other direction, it will move the scanning head along the page, stopping 300 times per inch, so it can scan 300 dpi in the other direction as well. This scanner would have an optical resolution of 300 x 300 dpi. Some manufacturers stop the scanning head more frequently as it moves down the page, so their machines have resolutions of 300 x 600 dpi or even 300 x 1200 dpi. Don't be fooled; what really counts is the smallest number in the grid. One can't get more detail by scanning more frequently in one direction only.

Interpolated Resolution: The other thing to watch out for is claims about interpolated or enhanced resolution. Unlike optical resolution, which measures how many pixels the scanner can see, interpolated resolution means how many pixels the scanner can guess at. Through mathematical interpolation, the scanner turns a 300 x 300 dpi scan into a

600 x 600 dpi scan by inserting new pixels in between the old ones, and guessing at what light reading it would have sampled in that spot had it been there. This process almost always diminishes the quality of the scan, and should therefore be avoided.

High quality art is often included in the submitted manuscript with low pixel resolution, sort of holding the space. Commercial printers do have scanners that operate at 1,200 or even higher pixels per inch. When the original art is sent along with the manuscript, the printer will scan the art with a high resolution scanner and inserts it where it belongs, replacing the low quality place-holder.

Electronic printers usually desire graphic files at no more than 600 dpi. Files with greater resolution are memory hogs.

Scanned text to be imported into publishing programs first must be processed through an Optical Character Recognition (OCR) program. OCR converts the graphic picture of a scan into readable characters. Optical character recognition has improved considerably over the past decade. Today, they not only correctly recognize 99 percent of the scanned text, but also proofread it, guessing at the correct word in case the recognition of one or more letters are doubtful.

High resolution scanners are very handy when it comes to OCR work. Small typefaces can be recognized much better at high resolution. Of course, if no high resolution scanner is available, one can enlarge the pages with a commercial xerox machine at Kinko's.

The two major OCR programs on the market are OmniPage® and TextBridge®. Both are available for PC's as well as for MacIntosh. Both are capable of handling foreign texts. They work with dozens of languages other than English, and are capable of recognizing two languages appearing on the same page. OmniPage is a lot more expensive than TextBridge, but, for example, it can recognize and correctly reproduce spreadsheet data and other tabular material. TextBridge can't handle such things, but with a good quality scanner it can perform wonders in recognizing text. OCR programs that are commonly bundled with low-end scanners do not give satisfactory results.

Proofreading a scanned and OCR-ed document is still very much required. One typical error, for instance, is the recognition of an apostrophe, such as in one's. Often the program assumes it is only a fleck of dirt, and neglects it. The 'Edit/ Find and Replace' function of the publishing program can correct this error by finding all "(space) s (space)" occurrences and replacing them automatically with 's (space).

OCR programs output their results directly into word processing programs, such a Microsoft Word or Corel WordPerfect. The result is often chock-full of formatting codes, switching font sizes, bold and normal typeface, and so on, throughout the text. WordPerfect's great advantage here with its 'Reveal Codes' function. When turned on, it shows all the hidden commands, font changes, hard carriage returns and other, often totally unnecessary marks. In most scanned and OCR-ed documents enormous numbers of such commands are hidden, bloating the files immensely. Rather than correcting all this garbage by using the 'Reveal Codes' function and eliminating the unnecessary coding step by step, it is often helpful to convert the whole text into ASCII Generic Word Processor or RichText (RTF) format to automatically eliminate the formatting codes. Once this is done, the text can be reconverted into the word processor application. But ASCII is not satisfactory for handling text in foreign languages where accented characters are present. It replaces them with blank spaces.

Scanning a document involves a great deal of manual work —boring work at that— but when compared to retyping a document, it is decidedly a winner.

In traditional printing, output to "camera ready copy" was the common requirement. With electronic book production, camera-ready output is replaced by Adobe Acrobat's Portable Document Format, or PDF. While the Acrobat Reader® program is free, writing to PDF requires the purchase of the full Acrobat program.

There are some hidden obstacles in the conversion of, for instance, a Ventura file into PDF. Some chapter tags, for example, are designed so that the new chapter starts on a right page. Ventura makes sure that there will be a left page in front of a new chapter, even if it is a blank page. Acrobat PDF, however, doesn't print a blank page, so the publication may end up missing a left page and placing a new chapter starting on a left side, with an odd-numbered page on it. To solve this problem, the writer must check the pages before each new chapter heading, and force a blank page before it, if necessary.

Corel Ventura 8	$ 470.00
Corel DRAW 9	$ 429.00
Corel Photo-Paint 9	$ 349.00
OmniPage Pro 10	$ 499.00
TextBridge Pro Millennium	$ 76.00
Adobe PageMaker 7.0	$ 499.00
Adobe Illustrator 10	$ 595.00
Adobe Photo-Shop 6.0	$ 609.00
Microsoft Publisher 2000	$ 100.00
Adobe In Design 1.5	$ 699.00
QuarkXpress 4.1	$ 780.00
Adobe Acrobat 5.0	$ 249.00

Prices of Publishing Software Packages

One of the major expenses in setting up a desktop publishing business is the cost of software. List prices, obtained from manufacturing company web sites, are shown in the table above. Of course, one needs only a few of these products. Most major suppliers offer their programs bundled together. For instance, Ventura includes Photo-Paint and WordPerfect. Similarly, the Adobe Publishing Collection contains PageMaker, Illustrator, Photo-Shop and Acrobat, and can be purchased for less than a thousand dollars, a modest price to spend on software to start up a book publishing program.

As discussed earlier, before the publishing process became completely digitized, the publisher had to provide "camera ready" copy to the printer. The commonly available laser printers are handy, until one desires to print out a whole book. Most home laser printers have limited memories.

After printing out 25 - 30 pages, they may choke. Printing a 400 page book by batches can become a chore. Fortunately, there are copy shops in most communities that are capable to handle such work at very reasonable rates.

Today, the work can be sent to the printer on a disk, using the "print to disk" command. One must know the type of imagesetter that the printing company uses in order to configure the printer setup[1] before executing the "print to disk" command.

While most cheap laser printers print at about 300 pixels per inch, commercial imagesetters print at over 1,200 pixels per inch. Some imagesetters used in magazine publishing print at over two thousand pixels per inch.

In book cover and dust jacket design color ink jet printers do come handy. Seeing one's design on paper, rather than on the computer's screen is advantageous. Ink jet printers are cheap. Some, in fact, are given away free with the purchase of a computer. The color reproduction of these low price printers is usually poor. A decent color printer could cost over $ 400, a dubious expense for a desktop publisher. It is more reasonable to let Kinko do the work.

---

1   Xerox printer drivers for personal computers can be downloaded from <www.fastcolor.com/postscript.html>

Marketing

The basic goal of a publisher is to make money. To accomplish this, first one has to produce books desired by readers. Once that is done, it has to be brought to the attention of the potential readers, whether through a bookstore, by direct sales, or through a library. In short, the book must be marketed.

The book market is enormous. In the year 2000 Americans bought 1.6 billion books, about the same amount than in the previous year. In 2000 about 67,000 titles were published. Ninety-four percent of these were bought from traditional stores. Six percent were bought online from stores like Amazon.com, Barnes&Noble.com and Borders.com, up from four percent in the previous year.

These appear to be formidable numbers, until one considers some other countries. In Britain, for instance, with one-fifth of the U.S. population, 100,000 titles were published in the year 2000.

In the process of deciding to publish a book and retire on the profits, at first one should consider the choice of the subject. An airline pilot's autobiography, even the lurid confessions of a stewardess, will not likely be a commercial success. In 1951, for instance, the most successful publication was *Betty Crocker's Picture Cook Book* put out by General Mills Corporation. In its year of publication, it outsold the best titles offered by the publishing trade by a factor of 5 to 1. In the year 2000 the same cook book was still in print, selling almost 100,000 copies in that year.

This number dwarfs when compared to the seven volume *McGuffey Reader*, an educational icon for a very long while, before fads swamped our public schools. It is now used in home schooling only. First published in 1838, an estimated 122 million copies have been printed of these books over the years.

Harlequin books, synonymous with syrupy romances and happy endings for a half-century, sold some four billion copies in that period. Its characters celebrated over 8,160 weddings in the process. Their publisher sells one out of six mass market paperbacks sold in North America, even though there are few people who would admit to their friends that they read fluff like that.

On the other end of the scale there are serious books written by famous people. Bill Clinton's 1996 book about his presidential agenda, *Between Hope and History*, sold fewer that 30,000 out of 180,000 printed. In 1990, former President Reagan received for his memoirs $ 8.5 million from Simon & Schuster. It turned out to be a publishing debacle. Hundreds of thousands were printed and less than 20,000 were sold. Likewise, after an $ 8 million advance, Pope John Paul II's memoirs barely sold, even in Catholic countries. On the other hand, Colin Powell's reported $6.5 million advance has probably paid off. It sold over one million hardcover copies. In 2001, Bill Clinton's unprecedented $10 million advance for his memoirs will be a risky venture, but certainly a monumental ego trip for everyone concerned.

Substance pays. David McCullough, who received the Pulitzer Prize for History for his biography of John Adams, tipped off the one million mark in book sales by the summer of 2001. His editor, Michael Korda — editor-in-chief of Simon & Schuster— stated that "its huge success is not only richly deserved but shows that people will read really good books in huge quantities if somebody will write them and somebody will publish them ... It may be, in fact, the first time ever a non-fiction work has outsold fiction on the summer bestseller list."

Most other books didn't fare as well. Those who did, like the Harry Potter stories, were the result of enormous media advertisement, costing millions of dollars.

Getting back to cook books, in the past 10 years major book publishers cut back the number of new cook book titles by half. According to *The Wall Street Journal*, the number of cook books entered into the International Association of Culinary Professionals' annual competition dropped 23 percent, to 335. One publisher specializing on cook books reportedly receives one-thousand cook book proposals a year. Only twenty of them make it to print.

Libraries are major markets for book publishers. These include academic, corporate and public libraries. There are over 4,000 college and university libraries in the United States. In addition, there are 16,241 public libraries, made up of 9,422 main libraries and 6,819 branch libraries. According to a 2001 *Library Journal* survey, average annual total materials budgets (books, videos, magazines, etc.) range from $33,000 for libraries serving populations under 10,000 to over $ 5 million serving metropolitan populations of 1 million or more. About 70 percent of the materials budget is spent on books.

The same survey indicated that for mid-size communities (100,000 - 250,000 patrons) materials budgets average just over $611,000 yearly. Mid-size communities spend the most on books — almost 80 percent, amounting to $479,000 a year. Multiplying the number of main libraries (9,422) with this number results in over $ 4.5 billion. This is the estimated aggregate yearly book budget of America's public libraries.

What kind of books do libraries purchase? According to experts, among the highest library expenditures on books are in the medical and health area, followed by fiction, arts/crafts/collectibles, biography, history and travel. A large part of these are in the reference areas. Surveys of librarians indicate that the most popular reference fields are social studies, including crime, social issues and law, how-to books, child care, development and rearing, health care and medicine, and business and management. Acquisition librarians are said to make their decisions on the basis of trade journals (some will be listed below), bestseller lists, wholesaler/distributor catalogs and specialty newsletters.

Fundamentally, there are two ways a small publishing firm can market its books:

> Establish a business relationship with a major publisher or a distributor company, in which the large firm handles all sales to the book trade for a fee. Generally, this fee ranges around 25 percent of the list price.

> Go it alone and try to maneuver though the bewildering array of national and regional wholesalers, both clicks and bricks and mortar booksellers, independent book stores, direct sales —either traditionally of through the Internet— and the endless maze of non-traditional markets.

The decision comes down to the question of economics and control. On one hand, it is convenient to lay back and wait for the monthly check. On the other, it may be better to make 25 percent on a smaller sales volume than 5 percent on a large one and meanwhile have a chance to improve the situation.

Whether or not to elect the contracted distribution option often depends on the profile of the small publisher. If its books focus on a small, well definable market, going alone may be the best way. But with titles that potentially interest a wide range of readers, national distribution companies may be the way to go. For an exclusive contract, these companies offer warehousing, cataloging, marketing, advertising, shipping, billing and collection. They all have nationwide distribution networks, experienced sales forces, and contacts with independent bookstores as well as with large chains. Some of the major book distributors in America are

National Book Network

4720 Boston Way

Lanham, MA 20706

www.nbnbooks.com

Publishers Group West

1700 Fourth Street

Berkeley, CA 94710

www.pgw.com

Independent Publishers Group

814 North Franklin St.

Chicago, IL 60610

www.ipgbook.com

Consortium Book Sales & Distribution

1054 Westgate Dr.

St. Paul, MN 55114

www.cbsd.com

Publishers who feel that they can do it as well as a major distributor, and save the fee to boot, need to learn about the marketplace. To reach this huge market, the primary reference book for a marketing person in book publishing is the *American Book Trade Directory*, a yearly publication put out by R. R. Bowker. According to to *The Huenenfeld Report*, it is "the most comprehensive and definitive guide available to the addresses, key personnel, and buying patterns of the key booksellers in the United States and Canada."

Bookstores sell books and some companies have a lot of bookstores. Here are a few addresses of major booksellers:

Barnes & Noble, Inc.

122 Fifth Avenue

New York, NY 10011

www.barnesandnobleinc.com

B. Dalton, Doubleday and Scribner's are subsidiaries of Barnes & Noble.

Borders Group Stores

100 Phoenix Drive

Ann Arbor, MI 48108

www.bordersgroupinc.com

is the major competitor of Barnes & Noble. Borders operates two groups of bookstores, Waldenbook Stores and Borders Books and Music.

Books-A-Million, Inc.

402 Industrial Lane

Birmingham, AL 35211

www.booksamillioninc.com

The latter operates 202 stores in 18 states, primarily in the Southeast.

Because they serve a captured audience, we mention college bookstores separately. The big one is

Barnes & Noble College Bookstores, Inc.

33 East 17th Street

New York, NY 10003

This firm operates about 1,200 stores, about one of every four American college bookstores. Their primary competitor is

Follett Higher Education Group

1818 Swift Drive

Oak Brook, IL 60523

This company operates about 660 stores. In addition to these two, there are a few smaller companies serving scores of college bookstores.

With the proliferation of computers with Internet access and online bookstores three companies stand out as leaders in online book selling. These are

www.Amazon.com

www.borders.com

www.booksamillion.com

www.bn.com

The last one stands for Barnes&Noble.com. In addition, one finds a number of smaller Internet bookstores, like

www.1Bookstreet.com

www.eCampus.com

www.A1Books.com

www.TextbookX.com

Apparently, these companies are highly competitive. Freeman's R. *E.Lee*, for instance, with a publisher's list price of $ 29.95, is available with UPS shipping included, anywhere from $29.95 to $39.94, plus sales tax, if applicable. Comparison-shopping is available through

www.AllBookstores.com

where some twelve Internet bookstores' prices and shipping costs are shown.

One of the advantages of online booksellers is that they do not have to stock every book that is on the market. However, their "virtual shelves" can display all the books that are in print. When an order comes, they arrange for shipping from their own or from their wholesaler's warehouse. A great advantage of online booksellers is that they can add short descriptions about their books, readers' ratings and review notes, assisting the potential buyers in the books' evaluation and selection. Somewhere on the bottom of the online catalogs there is a "publishers access" to do this.

Bookstores often show reluctance to set up a business relationship with a small supplier. Ordering, receiving, invoicing and so on for a few books each month is too much bother. It costs a great deal to set up a new vendor, for a small number of titles ordered each month, if any, it doesn't worth the trouble. Stores prefer to deal with a few, large suppliers, major publishers and the big, national wholesalers.

From the small publishers standpoint, dealing with small, regional wholesalers, jobbers, and small bookstores doesn't pay either. Taking orders, arranging for shipping, invoicing and collecting for a couple of titles at a time doesn't really worth it.

For any publisher, particularly a small one, establishing a business relationship with major wholesalers is essential. The major book wholesalers in America are:

Baker & Taylor Books, Inc.

501 S. Gladiolus Street

Momence, IL 60954

www.btol.com

Ingram Book Company

Nine Ingram Blvd.

La Vergne, TN 37086

www.ingrambookgroup.com

Book wholesalers do not sell directly to the public. Typically, an independent bookstore must agree to buy $10,000 worth of books each year to qualify for a business relationship with a wholesale house. For this reason, many independent book stores deal with either Ingram or Baker & Taylor, not with both. This is why publishers should establish a business relationship with both, in order to cover the market of small, independent bookstores.

It should be emphasized at this point that just because one has established business relationships with major wholesale houses, that, alone, will not sell books. Wholesalers do not advertise, they just fill purchase orders from bookstores and libraries. But serious marketing can start only after such relationship has been made.

The small publisher will need to advertise. That is the only way to reach the potential buyers, the reading public. The trick is, how and where.

Review magazines are the best vehicles to promote books at no cost before publication . We emphasize: *before publication*. A preliminary review copy of the book must be sent to these magazines at least three months before its review appears. Here are some review magazine addresses:

Library Journal

243 West 17th Street

New York, NY 10011

Kirkus Reviews

770 Broadway

New York, NY 10003

Booklist

P.O. Box 607

Mount Morris, IL 61054

Book News, Inc.

5739 NE Sumner St.

Portland, OR 97218

CHOICE

100 Riverview Center

Middleton, CT 06457

Publishers Weekly

245 West 17th Street

New York, NY 10011

New York Review of Books

1755 Broadway, 5th Floor

New York, NY 10019

The Barnes Review

130 Third Street S.E.

Washington, D.C. 20003

School Library Journal

245 W. 17th Street

New York, NY 10011

The last one's requirements rather well characterize the requirements of all others. Each year *School Library Journal* reviews some 4,000 children and young adult books, published as general trade or original paperback. The Journal requires a twelve week period before the book's date of publication. For submission, they want the publisher's catalog, two copies of the book, obviously in galley or page proof form, ISBN and LCCN numbers, author, title, binding, price and the month and year of publication. Their critique may be positive or negative, they could recommend for or against purchasing the book.

The other review magazines listed above all serve different markets. *Choice*, for instance, caters to academic librarians. *Book News* is aimed at librarians. Generally, for better success, it is advisable to look at a copy of the review magazine in question before contacting it, and compose the letter of submission to conform to their specific interest.

A bi-yearly publication, a free 48 page insert in California newspapers, carries numerous reviews of new books. It also displays advertisements from publishers. A typical 1/8 page sized ad costs $390. For this one reaches a circulation of 113,000 and an estimated readership of twice this number. The address is:

The Book Reader

245 Mt. Harmon Rd. # 256

Scotts Valley, CA 95066

To get noticed, many publishers send review copies of their books to the book editor of local newspapers. This is an expensive proposition. There are thousands of newspapers. Even if one counts only the major newspapers —say, those with weekday circulation exceeding 100,000— there are about 120 such papers in the United States. It is a lot to mail review copies to. Only a few of the books received by newspapers' book editors actually end up getting a published review. The same goes for sending a book to well-known columnists. On the other hand, once a book gets a review at one major newspaper it will probably be re-published at other papers as well. A good book review will entice many of the newspaper readers to go to the local bookstore and buy a copy.

Major publishers spend huge amounts of money to promote their recent issues. Tom Brokaw's *The Greatest Generation* had an advertising budget of $ 250,000. As part of the effort, the author went on a book-signing tour to dozens of cities in the nation. Another part of this budget is heavy advertisement in major newspapers and magazines.

The *New York Times' Sunday Book Review* is full of such ads. Most of them are from major publishers. The reason for this is simple. A one-time quarter page ad in the weekday editions of the *New York Times* costs $22,000, weekend rates are $26,200.[1] A regional paper would cost less, but would cover a much smaller market. For example, Florida's newspaper with the largest circulation,[2] the *St. Petersburg Times,* charges for a quarter-page ad in the Sunday book section $6,867. Even a quarter-page ad cost would be $3,433. All this for a one-time exposure to potential customers in the Tampa Bay area. A small publisher can not afford this type of advertisement. Experience shows that one-time ads are inferior to repetitive advertisements. In

1   The *New York Times* reported a 1,189,954 weekday and 1,698,281 Sunday circulation on 3/31/2001.

2   The *St. Petersburg Times* reported a 312,695 weekday and 396,557 Sunday circulation on 3/31/2001.

the language of advertisers, the number of "impressions" is important. The cost can add up rapidly.

There are specialty publications focused on books. The monthly *BookPage*, directed toward bookstore customers and library patrons, has a circulation of 650,000 and charges $3,600 for a half-page ad. The bi-monthly *Book Magazine* whose 250,000 subscribers are avid book readers, charges $2,700 for the same. The monthly magazine *Today's Librarian*, sent to 10,000 of the nation's public libraries, charges $830 for a half-page advertisement.

Small publishers may benefit from membership in the

Publishers Marketing Association

627 Aviation Way

Manhattan Beach, CA 90266

www.pma-online.com

This organization pools the resources of small publishers to provide periodic library mailings, targeted mailings to genre-specific booksellers, newsletters sent to approximately 3,700 independent booksellers, cooperative advertising, author road-shows and national book fairs. For an annual fee starting with $ 95, this could be beneficial for small publishers with limited financial resources.

There are marketing agencies that specialize on publishing promotion. Some of these are listed below, without endorsement, as we do not know them:

Marketing Directions

50 Lovely Street

Avon, CT 06001

Publishers Research and Marketing Company

1580 Lauderdale Lane

Bethpage, TN 37022

Publishers Support Services

P.O. Box 6698

Chandler, AZ 85246

Direct mail marketing of books is another promotional method directed toward librarians and booksellers. For mass mailings, R.R. Bowker developed an "outsert program," attaching book catalogs or flyers, shrink-wrapped together with their bi-monthly library mailing, or the annual mailing of *Books in Print*. The latter mailing, for instance, consists of 6,600 pieces and costs $ 2,178. Printing up that many promotional brochures or catalogs and shipping them to R.R. Bowker adds quite a lot to this cost. On the other hand, the catalog or brochure gets into the hands of acquisition librarians and bookstore buyers who make purchasing decisions.

It is worthwhile to mention here that the *Books in Print* database is said to power 65 percent of all library sales and over 50 percent of all wholesale and retail book sales.

www.Booksinprint.com

—a fee-based Internet service for book buyers at libraries and bookstores— had 37,000 unique users per month in the Fall of 2001. Bowker's Enhanced Listing Program allows publishers to create a link to their website from all their titles listed in the database, with a picture of the books' cover and a description (up to 200 words) of each title.

In direct mail marketing *targeted mailing* may have good results. This can be accomplished by first finding the proper niche (or niches) of a particular book. One such possibility is, for instance, is to target associations' membership lists or newsletters. Take, for example, a book dealing with home-based occupations. This, perhaps, of interest to associations of disabled persons. It is a big market. Approaching the editor of an appropriate newsletter with a proposal to include a reference to, or even better, to review and recommend the book to their members should contain a carrot: A part of the profit from the sales generated.Usually the profit on a deal is split evenly between the publisher of the book and the newsletter. It helps to read the mission statement of the organization before approaching it, to be fully aware of their interests and needs. For instance, a book on college education, like *The College Racket*, may be of interest to members of the AARP, since many grandparents support their grandchildren's college education financially, and they will be interested to know if their monies are well spent.

There are *list brokers* who rent lists for mailing. It is also common that newsletters rent their mailing lists to others for promotional purposes. Brokers have access to comprehensive lists to newsletters, professionals and fields of interests and activities, broken into regional groupings. List brokers, acting as "direct mail marketers" will aggressively promote their services in mass mailings, as much as 25,000 to 100,000 pieces. Direct mail marketing, such as these, can be quite costly. For this, standard procedure is to do a test mailing, for instance, 5,000 pieces to begin with. If the test mailing brings results, then they "roll out" with 25,000 or more.

For book promotion such mass mailings are chancy. It is better to proceed through the owners of the lists, the editors on associations that run the newsletters. Large newsletters, with 50,000 to 100,000 subscribers, are quite familiar with "stuffers." It is relatively easy to enlist their help in promoting a book if it is within their field of interest. Smaller newsletters — and there are a great many of them around— are less experienced with such deals, hence will require more subtle approach.

Experts in this field say that unendorsed solicitations through newsletters bring about one positive response in 200. Solicitations endorsed by the editors of the newsletter bring in up to one positive response in 20 solicitations.

One of the popular, yet economically not very rewarding sales method is book signing. Local papers list book

signings at neighborhood bookstores, where authors auto-
graph and dedicate books for their buyers. Major book
wholesalers make arrangements to ship adequate numbers
of books to these stores. This appear to be a greater benefit for the bookstore as it draws in potential buyers for
other books also.

Compared to the penny-ante approach to book selling, like
author appearances at bookstores, a company called

Advanced Marketing Services

5880 Oberlin Drive, Ste. 400

San Diego, CA 92121

www.advmkt.com

is doing marketing in a big way. Advanced distributes
books to the membership warehouse club industry, places
like Sams' Clubs, Costco and BJ's wholesale club stores,
shipping as many as 3 million books a week. Its invaluable
strength is their computerized sales database and software
program projecting what authors, genres and titles sell best
in which locations. The result is fewer titles returned unsold. Only a fifth of Advanced's books are sent back, versus past return experience of one in three. By essentially
outsourcing their book purchasing to Advanced, stores
carry the right amount of inventory. The upshot for Advanced is savings on unneeded store displays and on re-
turn-shipping costs.

One of the most significant venues of advertizing books
in the world are the traditional yearly book fairs of Frank-

furt, London, Chicago and San Francisco. Big publishers show, and sell, their new products on these occasions. Small publishers can not afford these. There are, however, local book fairs in some locations, often organized by local newspapers. Small publishers, or even single authors, may rent space for a couple of hundred dollars to show and sell their books.

The largest direct marketer of hardcover books in North America is

Books are Fun

P.O. Box 2468

1680 Highway 1 North

Fairfield, IA 52556

This company arranges book fairs and book display events at over 30,000 companies and 80,000 schools nationwide. They sell thousands, sometimes hundreds of thousands of copies of many books. They are very selective. Subject categories include cook books, children's storybooks, children's education, health, sports, hobby, reference nature, travel, inspirational and best selling novels and self-help titles. They are now owned by the Reader's Digest organization, which paid $ 300 million for the company.

Book clubs offer tremendous opportunities to increase sales. The best known is the *Book of the Month Club*, but there are over eighty others. Several specialty book clubs operate together, at the same address:

Book of the Month Book Club

1271 Avenue of the Americas

New York, NY 10020

Book clubs are very selective, but upon acceptance as much as 10,000 to 25,000 copies of the book could be sold. Even if a significant discount is to be given to the book club, it brings in a lot of cash.

Another method of promotion is when book marketers arrange television appearances for new authors. There are specialist companies who arrange these promotions.

The Internet offers a tremendous opportunity to advertize and sell books. Setting up a website and listing one's publications is neither too expensive nor is it difficult. One may list the books and provide a link to to one of the online bookstores. This is the so-called "Associate Program" that online bookstores offer. If they make a sale based on the linkage, they generally pay a five percent commission.

The more aggressive method of using a website is when one accepts Visa or MasterCard. There are such services on the Internet, so for a small fee one doesn't have to bother with the cards. Once the money is collected, the publisher can arrange shipment, either directly or by drop shipping from the printing company. Many printers or fulfillment companies will ship the books to the buyer from their plant or warehouse, usually in a plain box or envelope, to appear as if it came directly from the publisher.

Major publishers, marketing most of the major bestsellers, follow the performance of the market with keen interest. It drives their whole advertising programs. In the past, watching the *New York Times*' bestseller list, or *The Wall Street Journal*'s nationwide sales index, was very important. Since the advent of on-line book marketing, the Sales Rank of books on Amazon.com largely replaced the traditional methods.

It is an added service for customers, authors and publishers, showing how items in the Amazon.com catalog are selling. This bestsellers list is much like the *New York Times* bestseller list, except it lists thousands and thousands of titles. The lower the number, the higher the *sales rank* for that particular title.

The sales rank calculation is based on Amazon.com sales and is updated regularly. The top 10,000 best sellers are updated each hour to reflect sales sales of the preceding 24 hours. The next 100,000 are updated daily. The rest of the list is updated monthly based on several different factors. Barnes & Noble.com also shows sales rank in their online catalog. Even the major publishers check the position of their titles literally weekly on these on-line bookstores.

Lots of information about marketing books can be found in several Internet websites. Some of these are:

www.publishersweekly.com

www.bookmarketingprofits.com

www.publishingedge.com

www.bookpublishing.com

www.printingnews.com

http://publishing.about.com

R. R. Bowker's website includes publishers' homepages and their online catalogs. Its address is

www.bookwire.com

But getting on the R.R. Bowker Internet advertisement isn't cheap either. To display a book for a year the fee is about $ 400. For more books, there is a discount. For example, they advertise a dozen books for $1,200 on their website for a year. In contrast, the online bookstores not only advertise free, but also sell the books to the public.

To sum it all up, even if a small publisher has a very fine manuscript and produces an excellent book, bringing it to public attention is a difficult task that requires a great deal of attention, knowledge and effort, particularly if the advertising money is scarce.

The last word on this is *patience*. There are books that got on bestseller lists only after several editions, having first started out in a self published form. Here are a few examples:

What Color is your Parachute by Richard Nelson Bolles was first a self-published book. It went though 22 editions, 5 million copies and was on the *New York Times'* bestseller list for 288 weeks. Now it is published by Ten Speed Press in Berkeley, CA.

In Search of Excellence by Tom Peters was sold directly to readers in its first year. After selling over 25,000 copies, the book was bought by Warner Books which, in turn, sold 10 million more copies.

Leadership Secrets of Attila the Hun by Wess Roberts sold 486,000 copies before it was sold to Warner Books.

The One Minute Manager by Ken Blanchard and Spencer Johnson. They sold over 20,000 copies before selling the book to William Morrow Publishers in 1982. It sold 12 million copies since then. The book was translated into 25 languages.

The Celestine Prophecy by James Redfield. He self-published it and sold over 100,000 copies before he sold the rights to Warner Books for $800,000. Subsequently, the book was on the *New York Times* bestseller list for 165 weeks and became the number one bestseller in 1996. Over 5.5 million copies have been sold.

The Christmas Box by Rick Evans was also self-published. The 87 page book did so well that Evans sold it to Simon & Schuster for $ 4.2 million. It hit the top of the bestseller lists and was translated into 13 languages.

Mutant Message Down Under by Marlo Morgan was self-published and sold 370,000 copies before it was bought by HarperCollins for $ 1.7 million. Subsequently, it was taken up by to two book clubs, and the foreign rights was sold to 14 countries.

There are many other stories like these, but the reader probably got the message. One thing to point out is that these determined authors have used their own funds, as much as $ 10,000 or more at a time, to have their books printed. An independent publisher, using electronic printing and print-on-demand technology, can embark on the self-publishing business for a few hundred dollars.

Tracking a Copyright Owner

Unless one intends to publish only one's own writings —a rather tall order— publishing somebody else's work will require permission. The only exceptions to this are books that are in the public domain. Old books with expired copyrights are fair game. But if the copyright is still in force, the owner needs to be contacted before the book can be considered for publication.

This sounds simple. After all, there is the U. S. Copyright Office right at the Library of Congress, its address was given in an earlier chapter. The Copyright Office furnishes a report, for a fee, based on a search of their files for the current copyright owner, and whether the book is still covered by a copyright, or it is already in the public domain.

Before the changes in U.S. copyright laws in the 1978s and later the problem was simple: Was the copyright renewed 28 years after the book's initial publication? If the answer was yes, then 56 years after the publication date the book entered the public domain. But since the "author's life and fifty or more years" rule was introduced things got more complicated. Here are some examples:

Lowell Thomas wrote *Beyond Khyber Pass* and it was published by The Century Company in 1925. The copyright notice on the book's verso stated: "Copyright 1925 by The Century Co.". Mr Thomas died in 1981. Later it turned out that not Century or its corporate successors owned the copyright —that would have expired in 1981. The "Lowell Thomas Residuary Trust," administered by a New York law firm, holds the copyright and it shall do so until the 2020s. Is there a way to find out such information? Perhaps the Copyright Office might have the answer.

Carl Van Doren, famous American author, wrote his Pulitzer Prize-winning biography, *Benjamin Franklin* in 1938. The verso states: "Copyright 1938 by Carl Van Doren." The author died in 1950. Under the old rule, the copyright subsisted until 1994. But the "authors age" rule extended it to 2000. Did any changes made in the laws in the 1990s extended this copyright further? Only an attorney knowledgeable in the copyright laws would know.

The Copyright Office is not in the position to maintain up-to-date addresses of copyright holders. Searching the records of fifty states and countless foreign countries would take a monumental effort. Finding the right person or firm can be a daunting process. Here are a few examples:

Polish historian Oscar Halecki, author of *Borderlands of Western Civilization*[1] has immigrated to the United States after WW2 and published this book in 1952 while he was a professor at Fordham University. The publisher was The Ronald Press Company. According to the verso of an original copy of the book, Ronald Press Company held the

---

1   LCCN: 52-6197.

copyright. But by the time the search was made, Ronald Press was out of business. The Copyright Office search report indicated that the actual holder of the copyright was author Oscar Halecki, not Ronald Press.

To find information on Oscar Halecki, a search was made on-line on the Social Security Death Index

http://ssdi.geneology.rootsweb.com/cgi-bin/ssdi.cgi

Since the the time Social Security Law was enacted in 1936, Americans have to apply for Social Security cards and their time and place of death is registered in this index. In this case, it has shown that there was only one Oscar Halecki in the United States. He was born May 26, 1891, and he died in October, 1973 in White Plains, Westchester County, New York.

The search report of the Copyright Office also indicated that upon the expiration of the first term, the copyright was renewed in 1980 by Halecki's heir, Thadeusz Tchorzewski. The search was on for Tadeusz. He was not listed on the SSDI, hence he was either alive or he has left the United States. A search on the Internet Yellow Pages,

http://switchboard.com

showed that there were ten Tchorzewskis in America, but none of them had the first name Tadeusz. Were they heirs? Relatives? Acquaintances? A letter was sent to each, explaining the situation, with a SASE enclosed, requesting conformation that they are heirs of Tadeusz. Not a single answer came back. It is possible that there is a female relative under a married name, or that Tadeusz may have returned to his native Poland. The cultural attaché of the Polish Embassy in Washington offered help to find Tadeusz's relatives, though Polish - American newspapers and organizations, but nothing came from that effort either. Finally, an old friend of Halecki was found who could have helped, but he was in a nursing home suffering Altzheimer disease by that time, and was completely out of it. In the light of all this, it was decided to republish *Borderlands*, without formal approval by the copyright owner, with the provision of setting aside a customary and reasonable royalty against any potential future claims. As the book was produced on a print-on-demand basis, the worst possible outcome could be that the heir do not wish to cooperate. In this case the book can be taken out of print.

In the case of foreign authors whose occasional work was translated into English and published in the United States the problem is magnified. In some countries of Europe answering inquiries doesn't appear to be a priority at some publishers, even if one is lucky to identify them. For example, in the case of István Lázár, a Hungarian writer who personally sent his manuscript, *Transylvania, a Short History* to the author before his untimely death, it took well over a year to obtain a written permission from his publisher in Budapest.

Stalinist author Yuri Semyonov's *The Conquest of Siberia, an Epic of Human Passions* was written in the 1930s and was first translated into German in 1937. Later, it was translated into English and published in 1944 in London. Born in 1894, Semyonov was busy writing anti-American propaganda books until 1951. When and where he died is not known. Is *Siberia* in the public domain? Who would know the answer?

Ilya Ehrenburg (1891 - 1967) won a Stalin Prize with *The Fall of Paris* in 1942. Born in Kiev, his heirs, if any, could be anywhere in the former Soviet Union. His book is still under copyright protection under the "authors age plus..." rule. He was foreign correspondent in Paris for Moscow newspapers during the years he describes in his book. It could be considered a historical, cultural treasure. Should it be published without the copyright owners' permission?

In the case of Admiral Nicholas Horthy's *Memoirs*, another type of difficulty arose. In the early 1990s, the book was listed in *Books in Print* as available, in print. Originally, in 1957, it was printed by R. Speller, then, apparently was reissued by Greenwood Press in 1978,[2] quite without the knowledge of the heir of the copyright, Horthy's daughter-in-law, Mrs. Ilona Bowden, who lived in Portugal. When the title was ordered though a Borders bookstore, after several weeks of delay, the it was reported "unavailable." A search report by the U. S. Copyright Office has shown that the book's copyright was not renewed in 1975, hence now it was in the public domain. Still, republishing a book, even with a lot of alteration by added footnotes, wouldn't be reasonable as long as two publishers already indicate in *Books in Print* that the title is available. After lengthy correspondence with the publishers, the items

2   LCCN 57002991 and 78002681 respectively.

were supposed to be removed from a subsequent edition of *Books in Print.*

Upton Sinclair's books created a gargantuan problem. Much of his work appear to be in the public domain, *The Jungle,* for example, is published freely, but some other books where not. According to

www.findagrave.com

Sinclair died on November 25, 1968, at age 90, and was buried at the Rock Creek Cemetery in Washington, D.C.. The SSDI search confirmed his death date, birth date and Social Security Number, and that he died in Martinsville, Somerset County, NJ. A clue to Sinclairs' heirs was provided by his own writings, in one of the prefaces of his books. He wrote that his son David was at a boarding school in Germany just before WW1.

There were many David Sinclairs in the SSDI but only one matched: David Sinclair, born December 1, 1901, died on October 29, 1987 in Martinsville, NJ. Right age to be a school boy in Germany in 1913, also the right place of death. A letter to the Somerset County Surrogate's Court, after sending a fee of $ 3, produced a copy of David Sinclair's last will and testament. According to this document, he left his inheritance to a number of primary and secondary heirs. Every person named in the will have been subjected to an extensive search on the Internet. Addresses of identically named persons were collected and letters were sent, including a SASE, with appropriate inquiry. Only one person wrote back, indicating that she is not a relative at all. The trail went cold. Again, the decision was made to publish the titles that were still under copyright, with the provision to set aside potential royalties against later claims, if any.

Still more difficult is to locate copyrights belonging to defunct publishing companies. Some publishers fold outright, disappear without any trace. Others are bought up by larger publishing companies. In one case, for instance, when the new owner of a defunct company was clearly identified to be one of the largest publishing houses in the nation, months of correspondence and phone conversations with their legal department— even an appeal to the president of the firm that resulted in a benevolent response— led nowhere. The new owner had no record whatsoever of the rights, or even the title, of the publication sought.

Just because a fine book is under copyright protection, but has no clearly identifiable living owner, it should not be kept from the appreciating readers. After all, it is part of mankind's cultural heritage. Copyright infringement is wrong, it must be avoided at all cost, but does it apply to abandoned goods, much like a sunken ship? With a absent copyright owner is a copyright transfer to the state just like an abandoned savings account at a bank? Only the courts would know.

It seems reasonable, however, that if one republishes a title whose rightful owner is missing, paperwork should be kept, showing a good faith effort to find the owner. If a legal heir to the rights turns up, it is rational to assume that he or she will be reasonable in accepting a fair and customary royalty for all copies sold. If the offer is refused, the only sensible solution is to take the book off the market, therefore denying any future financial benefit to the owner of the copyright.

Hunting for Treasure

About 90,000 books go out of print each year. Many of them well deserve that fate. Perhaps they shouldn't have been printed to begin with. But there are books that are so valuable that they deserve to be kept in print for future generations. With traditional printing technology, keeping books in print economically was not possible. But print-on-demand changed that. Once the book was stored digitally, it would never be out-of-print.

How to select those really good books to be republished is a highly personal question. People's tastes in books are different. Popularity of titles also changes in time. Books that were on the bestseller lists some decades ago may be found out-of-date and boring today. But there are books that are enduring and timeless. Many were republished time and time again.

Conquest of Mexico, for example, by William H. Prescott (1796 - 1859) was first published in 1848. In the following fifteen decades this book was republished thirty times.

The Adventures of Hajji Baba of Ispahan by James J. Morier (1780? - 1849) was first published n 1828. Since that time the book was republished at least ten times. In 1954 it was even made into a motion picture. But, it is interesting to note that neither Morier's book nor Prescott's mentioned above were available at bookstores in the year 2000. Based on past history, someone was about to put them out again. There are many books like these. They keep coming back.

Old books, unavailable for many years, often find new life. For example, Victorian-age writer Anthony Trollope (1815 - 1882) —under whose name 362 titles come up in the online catalog of the Library of Congress— has gone through a revival 100 years after his death. First came the popular BBC serial, *Pallissers* in 1974, followed by the oh-so-scholarly exhibition of his works at Princeton University, then his 1883 *Autobiography* was republished in 1996. Scores of Trollope's books can be found in the online catalog of Amazon.com today, most of them with five-star rating.

Out of Africa, a memoir written in 1937 by Danish writer Karen Blixen (1885 - 1962), was out of print for decades. Then, nearly a half a century later, it was turned into a popular movie by Sydney Pollock in 1985. The film was judged to be a masterpiece. Then, in the year 2000, the title reappeared as a TV documentary film in Great Britain.

English Patient, a 1992 novel by Michael Ondaatje was about the life of Hungarian Count László Almásy (1895 - 1951). Almásy, a pilot/geographer, was a noted Sahara expert, who, for instance, found 8,000 year old cave paintings in the Gilf-el-Kebir mountains in Western Egypt. As a Hungarian army officer during WW2, he was seconded to Rommel's Army as an advisor. Ondaatje's book was turned into a screenplay in 1996, then a blockbuster film in in 1997 that won nine Oscars, among them the Best Picture Award. It was a tear-jerking love story. But in reality, the good Count had an unconventional sexual orientation and he also survived the war, only to die of typhoid fever in 1951. His 1940 book about his experiences, *With*

Rommel's Army in Lybia[2], was first published in English in 2001.

Some extraordinary books, on the other hand, disappear from the shelves of bookstores for decades. With electronic printing, this should not be so anymore.

James Truslow Adams (1878 - 1949), for instance, was one of the greatest American historians. He wrote a number of outstanding books on the colonial period of North America, on New England, and on the founding fathers. Although he won a Pulitzer Prize in History, fifty years after his death all but one of his books were out-of-print for many decades. What an utter waste of knowledge!

Identifying Lost Treasures

There is a great deal of very valuable material, like the books just mentioned, among long-out-of-print titles. To find them takes some effort. First, one needs to identify them. In the case of fiction, there are helpful books to assist in this. One of them, for example, is

Martin Seymour-Smith: *Who's Who in Twentieth Century Literature*, Holt, Rinehart and Winston, 1976

There are many other guides like this, both in print and on the Internet. Many of the books listed in these guides are

---

2   Translated by Gabriel Francis Horchler, Bloomington: 1st Books, 2001.

out-of-print, their copyright term expired, they are in the public domain.

Some of the best of these books won literary awards. To find out about such things, the search should start with

www.literature-awards.com

A similar website is

www.stat.wharton.upenn.edu/~siler/litlists.html

Pulitzer Prize winners can be located on

www.pulitzer.org

An extensive worldwide listing of authors of literary value is the Finnish site:

www.kirjasto.sci.fi/indeksi.htm#a

Once a book is identified as a potential reprint, one should check it if it is really off the market. There is little reason to reprint a book that is still in print. Determining this is easy to do. Amazon.com's online catalog lists just about every book that was ever published. It spells out clearly if the book is "hard to find" or "out-of-print." Barnes&Noble.com does it too.

Once a title is found to be out-of-print, the next task is to check its publishing history. To learn about a book, or an author's publishing history, one should visit the on-line catalog of the Library of Congress. Its address is:

http://catalog.loc.gov/

This catalog is available 24 hours a day. It may be searched by subject, author's name, book title or library call number. Searching by the author's name is the best to start with. It tells not only when the book was originally published but also when it was republished and by whom. The author's other publications listed there as well. These may become potential new publications.

Some books cannot be found by their author's name. This often happens with foreign publications. In such a case, a title search is in order.

Man of Glory: Simón Bolívar by Thomas Rourke is an appropriate example. This fine 1939 book was not listed under the author's name, as if he never existed. Checking it under the title, the book showed up. But the real author turned out to be Daniel Joseph Clinton. Thomas Rourke was a pseudonym. God knows why.

The Library of Congress online catalog is a good lead to find other publishable titles. For instance, one often finds co-authors' names. Co-authors may have fine, publishable books listed under their own names.

One important data about a book is the control number, which is provided by the Library of Congress catalog. Often a book was published in Great Britain as well as in the United States. Knowing the right LCCN for a copy at hand is needed when the new ISBN number is assigned. Today the LCCN is shown on the verso of a book but it was not necessary in the past.

Getting a Copy

Once a prospective reprint title is identified, one needs to find a copy somewhere. In the past, it was a gargantuan problem. Even in the recent past, searching for an old, long out-of-print book involved going to an antiquarian bookstore, preferably in an old college town or in New York, Boston and similar cultural centers. Overseas, in London, Zurich, Geneva, Paris, Rome and other major European capitals and university towns chances to find some literary gems were even better. But who can afford traveling overseas to browse the dusty shelves of out-of-way antiquarians on the remote chance to find a specific book? There wasn't even a list of addresses available to write inquiring letters to used book stores. There were a few specialists around who offered help in locating obscure titles, but generally the outlook was bleak. Not anymore.

Next to electronic print-on-demand technology, perhaps the most significant development involving the publishing industry is the on-line search capability of the catalogs of antiquarian bookstores. Efforts to bring the power of the Internet to the old book marketing business started in around 1996. Computerizing databases for bookstore inventories took a long time. But by late 2001, one electronic book-searching service,

www.BookFinder.com

boasted over 30,000 different booksellers, worldwide, on a single search engine. Another, the Advanced Book Exchange

www.ABEbooks.com

claims to have over 8,400 stores that sell antique, used books linked to its search engine. Books can be defined by title, author, keywords, ISBN, paperback or hardcover, first edition or signed copy and so on. Once located, the book may be purchased online from the bookseller, or directly from Advanced Book Exchange. Many stores accept credit cards online.

Similar used book-finder websites are:

www.bibliofind.com

www.Alibris.com

www.TomFolio.com

www.Biblion.com

www.Antiqbook.com

www.JustBooks.com

The last three on this list are European-based, specializing in second-hand and antiquarian books.

While these search engines are said to be interconnected, it is advisable to check with more than one search engine to find a book. Also, even if the same title is available at several bookstores, there are considerable variations in price. One may find a title at two different search engines, one for $50, another for $60, the third search engine may locate a perfectly fine copy for $12.

It is an exhilarating experience to find, for example, the single surviving copy of a book in a bookstore in Sidney or in Stockholm. Furthermore, the fact that this almost extinct book may cost no more than $20 including shipping defy one's imagination. Not many years ago locating the single remaining copy of a title, sitting on a shelf in a little foreign bookstore was unimaginable.

It may happen that one finds a century-old book with its pages uncut, but some old books are badly marked up with notes and under-lining, in ink. In case of doubt, it is advisable to ask the bookseller before placing an order, to check if the pages are clean of under-linings, spots and dirt, and scannable for reproduction. Most antiquarian books are returnable, but still, it is good to ask before ordering.

In republishing an old book that is in the public domain, or the the holder of the copyright allows the use of the book in return of agreed royalty, the publisher has two choices. One choice is to completely re-scan the book, using a character recognition program and a publishing software. It is a lot of busywork, and it may still leaves a great deal of typographic errors in the final manuscript. On the other hand, it will result in a clear, modern typographic design and setup. Such material can be edited, footnoted, combined with other texts and so on.

Another choice is to provide a clean original copy to the electronic printer, who will scan the entire book on a high-speed scanner. In this case the publisher will have to provide a new title page and a new verso, with the original publishing information as well as the new ISBN and new publisher's data shown.

The cost of placing a title in the electronic library of a printer is significantly cheaper when the text is submitted in digital form. Scanning a hard copy is as much as three times more costly than digital submission. On the other hand, reproducing an existing book digitally is a lot more work, particularly if it is full of tables and illustrations.

Some old, nineteenth century books have fragile pages. These must be scanned on a flat-bed scanner by hand, requiring special handling at an extra charge.

In both cases, the new cover pages, and, in the case of a hardcover book, the dust jacket design will have to be furnished. Knowledge of Adobe Photo-Shop, Corel Photo-Paint or another graphic software helps to take care of this requirement. Finding suitable cover art is easy, if one searches the Internet. There is a large amount of potentially useful illustrations available, most without copyright protection.

An Example

In the year 2001, the author, under the name of Simon Publications Inc. have published a considerable number of history books that were similar in many ways: They all were out-of-print for decades, they were bestsellers at their time of publication, many were written by Pulitzer Prize-winning authors or by people of world renown. Currently, there are nearly 200 titles in this collection. More high-quality books are to be added to the list every month, as soon as they are located.

These titles were selected with a great deal of care. The first step in searching for worthy books was the list of titles that won Pulitzer Prizes in history and in biography. Titles published after WW2 looked, potentially, to be still under copyright protection. Earlier titles were likely to be in public domain, particularly if their authors died before the middle of the century. In some doubtful cases the Copyright Office was contacted for information. In cases when the title definitely appeared to be still under copyright protection, a search was made for the author or his or her surviving heirs. With those that were identified —in some cases the publisher, in others the author or his heirs— a letter-form publishing agreement was executed.

Pulitzer Prizes were first awarded in 1917. This and the year 1945 bracketed a certain number of books. Some of them were found to be still in print. Those were taken off the list. Others were judged out of style, with precious little readers' interest these days. They too were dropped from the list.

After the final list was made, the authors' other works were reviewed. In the case of John Truslow Adams, for example, this provided many new leads. Some of these books had coauthors, their names were checked also.

The cheapest, but best preserved, copies of the selected titles were located on the Alibris.com or ABEbooks.com catalogs and purchasing decisions were made. With relatively few exceptions the cost of these books, including shipping, ranged between $ 20 to $ 40.

Once purchased, the bibliography and references listed in the books were scrutinized for other potential targets. For instance, Millin's *General Smuts* made very frequent references to Lloyd George's voluminous *War Diary*. That, too, proved to be an excellent potential publication. Sure enough, less than a month after its publication, it was extensively quoted in a new book, Wolfson, R & John Laver: *Years of Change*, London: Hodder & Stoughton, 2001.

Once the selection of books reached world-wide coverage, some gaps in territorial coverage were noticed. For example, a good book was needed on the Khmer Empire and one on the history of Thailand. There are antiquarian bookstores around that specialize in certain geographical areas. Most used book sellers are very cooperative in giving advice on these topics. They provided excellent leads.

Even though a great deal of work went into selecting the best, most reliable and informative titles, some of the books purchased turned out to be duds. Even with the best intentions, as much as ten percent the books bought had to be thrown out. An unnecessary expense? No. Strict weeding assured that the remaining books were top quality. There was another limitation, the price. Some antiquarian books are just way too expensive. For instance, G. A. Henty's *The March to Magdala*, published in London in 1868 —describing the 1867 military expedition led by General Sir Robert Napier to rescue British diplomats imprisoned by the Ethiopians— is offered for $3,950 by a Vermont antiquarian. Probably it is a fascinating book, but couldn't be republished at that cost.

In some cases, books could not be located anywhere. For these, some search firms, like Alibris, offer individualized searches. For instance, even using some of these services, it has taken almost six months to locate a copy of C. A. Macartney's *Hungary and her Successors* at a used book store in Stockholm. It was marked up a bit, but a good eraser and some white-out paint did wonders. There were some others like this. Lawrence Cramer's 1929 book, *The Diplomatic Background of the World War* was entirely unavailable. Not a single copy of this thin 132 page paperback was to be found anywhere in the world. Finally, personal contacts led to a retired professor of political science who had a copy, with yellow fluorescent Hi-Lighter markings all over. Luckily, the scanner didn't see it.

Ultimately, the books were sorted into the following collections:

American History
European History
Latin American History
Near Eastern History
African History
Oriental History and Cultures
World Religions
Historical Fiction
General Interest

The focus of the European collection was World War I, its causes and its consequences. This stemmed from the notion that most of the ills of Europe— all the *isms* of the twentieth century— were ultimately rooted in the flawed Paris Treaties at the end of the Great War. Most of the titles collected were written by contemporary statesmen and diplomats, who were participants on one side or another. These books contain primary historical source material, not a rehash infused by propaganda. In the process of searching, we stumbled on a few other titles, like Maurois' *Disraeli* and Oliveira Martins' *Prince Henry the Navigator* — the founding father of colonialism —that we couldn't resist.

Even though the Africa collection contains few books, on the whole, it provides a remarkably thorough coverage of the history of the continent. Two books were exceedingly hard to find: Bettany's 1890 *The Dark Peoples of the Land of Sunshine* , and Sanderson's 1907 *Great Britain in Africa, the History of Colonial Expansion.*

There were some overlaps in the groupings of these books. *Prince Henry the Navigator* could have been listed as part of the Africa collection, for instance.

Oriental history and cultures are tremendously wide subjects. Without the marvelously rich bibliography of Gunther's *Inside Asia* —covering the region from Tel Aviv to Tokyo and from Siberia to Siam— the collection would have been much poorer.

There is an enormous wealth of information in books that were published in the nineteenth century. For example, the 1,600 page *The Middle Kingdom* by Williams is still a great reference on China's history and culture, even though it was written in 1882. Three early nineteenth century books, *Chinese Characteristics, Hajji Baba of Ispahan,* and *Hindu Manners* give a delightful characterization of the typical Chinese, Persian, and Indian, in a penetrating manner. They would not pass a politically correct copy editor's muster in our non-judgmental, multi-cultural era today. Yet their depicted objects —at least the Iranians and the Hindus— still consider these books as entirely valid characterizations of themselves, and they make sure that these books stay in print, at least in Tehran and New Delhi.

The quality of the selected titles has shone through the appreciation of the readers. Many titles gained top, five star ratings on Amazon.com reader evaluation reports only a few months after they appeared on the market. It is also interesting to note the wide range of the popularity of these titles. For instance, it was totally surprising and unexpected that Breasted's *The History of Egypt* would turn out to be one of the bestsellers among these titles.

As more and more books entered the market during 2001 readers' preferences became noticeable. Historical novels by Erich Maria Remarque and C. S. Forester sold well. As a result, more titles by these authors were identified, purchased and published. Soon after publication many of these titles received four or five star rating by readers on the online bookstore of Amazon.com.

Purchasing and setting these books up in the printer's computer database was not an expensive proposition, about $200 per book. A few, like Kelemen's *Medieval American Art*'s second volume, containing over 900 photographs of pro-Columbian art, required special handling to minimize moiré effects at a cost well exceeding $2,000. Even though this investment is unlikely to be reclaimed, reprinting a title like that improved the quality of the whole collection.

The book collection is described in detail on the website:

www.SimonPublications.com

There are some 200 books shown on this website. The information provided includes a picture of the cover, a short description of the book, its original date of publication, ISBN number, page count and list price. The collection is searchable alphabetically by author and by title. The twelve page hard copy catalog is downloadable in PDF format.

Index